The Psychodynamics of and Modern Horror Ci

In this illuminating volume, Carlos Pitillas and Ismael Martínez-Biurrun provide in-depth analysis of contemporary horror films from a psychoanalytic perspective.

Drawing on Freudian psychoanalysis, object relations theory and relational psychoanalysis, the authors explore the ways in which horror films present different aspects of traumatic phenomenology and the re-emergence of unprocessed traumatic wounds. Covering films as diverse as *Psycho, The Babadook, Black Swan,* and *A Nightmare on Elm Street*, the authors dissect the use of symbolism and metaphors in popular horror cinema to show how the disruptive threats faced by characters in these films often function in the same way as post-traumatic stress disorder, and consider behaviours such as repetitive thoughts and actions, dissociation, and more through the lens of neuroscience and narrative theory.

This book is an important and novel read for all psychoanalysts in practice and training looking for new ways to understand and work with clients who have experienced traumatic life events. The authors' use of familiar and canonical horror films also equips students and researchers of film studies with the knowledge necessary to integrate psychoanalytic theories into their work.

Carlos Pitillas is an associate professor and researcher in the department of Psychology at Comillas Pontifical University, Spain. He is a psychotherapist working with children, adolescents, and adults. His interests focus on early socioemotional development and attachment relationships; relational trauma and its intergenerational transmission; interpersonal psychoanalytic psychotherapy; and intersections between psychology and popular culture. His current teaching covers developmental psychology, psychoanalysis, psychoanalytic psychotherapy, and child and adolescent psychotherapy. He is the Director of the upcoming master's degree in Psychoanalytic Contemporary Psychotherapy at Comillas Pontifical University.

Ismael Martínez-Biurrun is an award-winning novelist, creative writing teacher, and adjunct lecturer at Comillas Pontifical University, Spain. He has published nine novels and has had his work included in several short story anthologies. His work combines psychological thriller with horror and urban fantasy.

The Psychodynamics of Trauma and Modern Horror Cinema

I Am What Haunts Me

Carlos Pitillas and
Ismael Martínez-Biurrun

Routledge
Taylor & Francis Group
LONDON AND NEW YORK

Designed cover image: Getty Images © WIN-Initiative/Neleman

First published 2025
by Routledge
4 Park Square, Milton Park, Abingdon, Oxon OX14 4RN

and by Routledge
605 Third Avenue, New York, NY 10158

Routledge is an imprint of the Taylor & Francis Group, an informa business

© 2025 Carlos Pitillas and Ismael Martínez-Biurrun

The right of Carlos Pitillas and Ismael Martínez-Biurrun to be identified as authors of this work has been asserted in accordance with sections 77 and 78 of the Copyright, Designs and Patents Act 1988.

All rights reserved. No part of this book may be reprinted or reproduced or utilised in any form or by any electronic, mechanical, or other means, now known or hereafter invented, including photocopying and recording, or in any information storage or retrieval system, without permission in writing from the publishers.

Trademark notice: Product or corporate names may be trademarks or registered trademarks, and are used only for identification and explanation without intent to infringe.

British Library Cataloguing-in-Publication Data
A catalogue record for this book is available from the British Library

Library of Congress Cataloging-in-Publication Data
Names: Pitillas Salvá, Carlos, author. | Martínez Biurrun, Ismael, 1972- author.
Title: The psychodynamics of trauma and modern horror cinema : I am what haunts me / Carlos Pitillas and Ismael Martínez-Biurrun.
Description: Abingdon, Oxon ; New York, NY : Routledge, 2025. | Includes bibliographical references and index. |
Identifiers: LCCN 2024037586 (print) | LCCN 2024037587 (ebook) | ISBN 9781032703497 (paperback) | ISBN 9781032743790 (hardback) | ISBN 9781003468981 (ebook)
Subjects: LCSH: Horror films--History and criticism. | Psychoanalysis and motion pictures. | Psychic trauma in motion pictures. |
LCGFT: Film criticism.
Classification: LCC PN1995.9.H6 P53 2025 (print) |
LCC PN1995.9.H6 (ebook) | DDC 791.43/6164--dc23/eng/20241007
LC record available at https://lccn.loc.gov/2024037586
LC ebook record available at https://lccn.loc.gov/2024037587

ISBN: 978-1-032-74379-0 (hbk)
ISBN: 978-1-032-70349-7 pbk)
ISBN: 978-1-003-46898-1 (ebk)

DOI: 10.4324/9781003468981

Typeset in Times New Roman
by KnowledgeWorks Global Ltd.

Contents

List of figures   *viii*

Introduction   1

*Three traumatized characters, and the monsters that
   speak for them 1
Trauma, storytelling, and horror films 3
This book 5*

1 Traumatic disruption in modern horror cinema   7

*Trauma as a disruption of basic trust 8
Three traumatic fractures in horror narrative 9
   The self and the body 9
   Others and relationships 14
   The world or cosmos 16
Unpeeling, awakening, dis/ease 18
Trauma as a disruption in the processing of experience 20
   Predictive processing and metaphor 20
   Freeze to survive 21
   Silencing, shaming, and failure of recognition 24
Trauma as a disruption in the registering of experience 26
Symbols of the immutability of trauma 30*

2 Traumatic fragmentation in modern horror cinema   33

*A disconnect between memory and perception 33
   Clotted affect and other resistances 36
Post-traumatic fragmentations of identity (I): Survival by
   self-division 39*

Post-traumatic fragmentations of identity (II): Dividing others to preserve them 45
Uninvited guests 47

3 Modes of traumatic re-emergence in modern horror cinema   50

Brain hijacking: The tyranny of the limbic system 55
Pain without language: Narrative collapse and muteness 56
Inhabiting an alternative language 58
Caught in the primary process 60
  Disjointed time 61
  Contradiction and allegorical moment 62
Repetition and its masks (I): Suffering from reminiscences 66
Repetition and its masks (II): Acting out the wound 69
A Gothic nightmare: The transmission of trauma between generations 72
  Paradoxes of traumatic parenthood in three horror films 75

4 The hero's darkest journey: Trauma storytelling in modern horror film   79

Two models of storytelling 80
A possible structure of horror 81
  Sightings 82
  Resistance 85
    No sheriff, no father: The dissolution of authority 87
    A failure of language 88
  Acceptance 90
    The role of the shaman 91
    Naming the monster 93
  Trance 95
    A voluntary sacrifice: Turning your back on Freddy 96
    Retrieve the body/Catch the monster 98
    The triumphant smile of trauma 101

5 Reclaiming the metaphor, embracing the monster: Using horror films in psychotherapy with traumatized patients   105

Three approaches to the use of horror films in psychotherapy 106
Iconic language and formulation of experience 107

Moving within the window of tolerance 109
Moving in the transitional space 110
Allegorical moment and the transition from dissociation to conflict 111
Embracing the monster: Identification and reappropriation of trauma-related contents 113
Putting the characters on the couch 114
Coda 115

References *116*
Index *126*

Figures

0.1 In *It Follows* (Mitchell, 2014), Jay is followed by shifting destructive presences that represent a traumatic relationship with her father.   3

1.1 In *The Brood* (Cronenberg, 1979), Nola's psychic pain emerges in the form of bodily transformations, particularly a strange baby, born of out Nola's post-traumatic rage.   13

1.2 *The Babadook* (Jennifer Kent, 2014) depicts the traumatic transformation of a nurturing, protecting figure into a monstrous source of threat.   16

2.1 In *Black Swan* (Aronofsky, 2010), Nina faces a dark transformation (see the blackness spreading over her arm) related to the division of her psyche.   42

2.2 In *Spider* (Cronenberg, 2002), Denis deals with relational pain and confusion by dividing the representation of his mother into two opposing images, as well as by obsessively creating web-like structures that help him keep his psychic balance.   46

3.1 In *His House* (Weekes, 2020), strange presences move behind the walls, bringing with them the memory of a traumatic migration story suffered by its protagonists.   55

3.2 In *Psycho* (Hitchcock, 1960), Norman transformation into his aggressive mother manifests as a contradictory, disjointed, allegorical moment of confusion between past and present, fantasy and reality, self and other.   65

4.1 In *The Exorcist* (Friedkin, 1973), Regan's mother has to overcome all of her rational resistances and finally accept her need of another kind of help.   90

4.2 In the climax of *A Nightmare on Elm Street* (Craven, 1984), Nancy not only dares to confront Freddy Krueger directly, but she even turns her back on him to prove she is no longer afraid, thus nullifying his power.   97

4.3 At the end of *Midsommar* (Aster, 2019), Dani's face turns from a pained grimace to an unhinged smile: far from signifying a triumph or an overcoming, this smile suggests a definitive fall into the abyss of trauma.   103

Introduction

Three traumatized characters, and the monsters that speak for them

After having sex with her boyfriend, Jay – the protagonist of *It Follows* (Mitchell, 2014) – discovers that by sleeping with her, he has passed on a very particular curse: an undefined presence or entity (which in the film is simply called "It") will follow her until it kills her, or until she herself can pass on the curse to a new sexual partner. The film shows Jay's efforts to escape the danger that haunts her. Several people die along the way and Jay's paranoia grows as "It" is able to take on the appearance of any person. The plasticity of the threat, its insidious nature, and the absence of a rational explanation for its existence force us to reflect on its possible relationship with the intrapsychic: what is it that really haunts Jay? Is it a coincidence that the entry of this threat into her life coincides with a sexual relationship? Although *It Follows* moves within an elegant ambiguity, its climax seems to suggest that the monster does, in fact, have a traumatic significance. Jay and her friends stage an ambush of sorts in an indoor swimming pool, determined to put an end to the menace once and for all (the intention, specifically, is to lure it into the water and electrocute it). Then, in what seems to us to be its last appearance, the monster takes on the form of someone recognizable to Jay: it appropriates the features of her absent father (whom we recognize from a Polaroid shown at the beginning of the film). We do not know his whereabouts, why he is missing, or what kind of relationship he had with his wife and daughters. We only know that the sight of him makes Jay tremble, and that his presence concludes the persecution that she has been facing since she had her sexual encounter. We wonder, then, if this supernatural threat metaphorizes the re-emergence of an unprocessed experience of abuse or mistreatment at the hands of her father.

Annie, the protagonist of *Hereditary* (Aster, 2018), is a mother struggling to avoid a legacy of madness and destructiveness that has circulated in her family through the generations. Schizophrenia, suicide, and other forms of self-destructiveness, she confesses in a self-help group, run through her veins. Annie is especially haunted by the memory of her relationship with her enigmatic and very hostile mother, whose footsteps she is afraid to follow. A specific strategy serves to keep the madness at bay: the creation of scale models of scenes from her own life. Her workshop is filled with small reproductions of episodes featuring her children, her mother, or herself. By recreating them and encapsulating them in a miniaturized version, Annie acquires a certain control over experiences that, in real life, are marked by a very threatening vulnerability. These reproductions represent Annie's efforts to maintain her psychic balance and to curb the intergenerational pull of trauma. However, the accidental death of her daughter sets in motion a process of disorganization that leads Annie to transform herself into a monstrous and destructive mother, capable of setting her husband on fire and sacrificing her surviving son to a cult that worships a satanic deity. The ghosts of the traumatic relational past have become present, turning Annie into a replica of her own mother and destroying her bonds with her husband and son.

Oskar, the protagonist of *Let the Right One In* (Alfredson, 2008), is an inhibited and lonely boy who is bullied at school. His parents, absorbed by a painful divorce and emotionally disconnected from him, are unaware of Oskar's suffering and unable to protect him, as are other authority figures (mainly teachers) who, by omission, are complicit in the abuse he suffers. In the privacy of his bedroom, Oskar fantasizes about taking violent revenge on his attackers and collects newspaper clippings reporting murders in his town. One night Eli, a strange girl who appears to be the same age as him, enters his life. We soon discover that Eli is a vampire. Her strange roommate (a kind of protector) murders fellow citizens and collects their blood to feed her. While Oskar secretly gathers news about violent affairs, Eli and his partner kill innocent people, in a disturbing parallelism that lends itself to a psychological reading: Eli is a representation (supernatural, and perhaps fantasized) of Oskar's post-traumatic rage, of his resentment towards a hostile and indifferent world. As well as representing Oskar's unformulated rage, the vampire is the first source of human contact that our protagonist finds in a cold world, where it is always night, and where his parents are not available to him. Eli progressively becomes Oskar's friend and channels his anger by enacting revenge on his aggressors. A final scene shows Oskar in a train compartment, travelling away from his city. His luggage consists of a big box, inside which Eli protects herself from the daylight.

These three stories share themes that are at the heart of this book. They all feature someone who has been the victim of a painful and unprocessed experience: a possible sexual abuse, a toxic relationship with an abusive mother, a bullying situation. In all three cases, these victims have lacked a containing environment or 'relational home' (Atwood & Stolorow, 2014) to help metabolize their experience and regulate the painful emotions resulting from these harms, or a witness (Benjamin, 2018; Herman, 2015) that may account for the victimization and position themselves morally close to the victims. They are all haunted by supernatural presences that metaphorize the trauma: Jay is followed by shifting destructive presences; Annie herself becomes the mother-monster; Oskar encounters a reflection of his destructive rage and – better off than the other characters – learns to live with it. In all cases, the re-emergence of the unprocessed takes the form of something monstrous.

Figure 0.1 In *It Follows* (Mitchell, 2014), Jay is followed by shifting destructive presences that represent a traumatic relationship with her father.

Trauma, storytelling, and horror films

The human species is a fragile one. We are creatures vulnerable to aggression from our natural environment and – even more frighteningly – from our fellow humans. Our current brain is the result of thousands of years of evolution in a context marked by scarcity, the need to migrate, competition for resources and sex, high mortality, or vulnerability to predators (Quammen, 2004); it is an organ that carries a core learning which guides much of our behavior: *you are vulnerable; you are meat.*

Our reflexive capacity requires that experiences of pain and danger take place in two different moments: there is an original, raw impact, and then there is the need to process and represent that impact. It is no wonder that, since the birth of culture, poets and philosophers have tried to use words and ideas to symbolize suffering and make it more legible. More recently, in the transition between the 19th and 20th centuries, the concept of *trauma* (which comes from the Greek for 'wound') has become a new intellectual tool with which we have been trying to make sense of human pain.

The horror genre (in both literature and film) is a fertile ground for the representation of the traumatic. From the earliest Victorian Gothic fiction to today's 'elevated horror', the horror stories we are told are often about a painful, unintegrated past that tends to return. This twinning of psychological trauma with narrative horror is probably not a historical accident. There is essentially something *monstrous*, a "supernatural" (Monk, 2023) feel to the way in which post-traumatic symptoms make their way into people's lives. The repetition of early trauma within affective relationships (Gleiser, 2003), re-experiencing in the form of flashbacks and intrusive memories (van der Kolk, 2015), and repetitive dreams and play found among traumatized children (Perry and Szalavitz, 2017; Terr, 1990), all share a phenomenology based on 'exteriority': they are experienced as something alien, foreign, that invades the victim's mental life. Within horror cinema, the monster is seldom recognized by protagonists as something belonging to their past or their self: it is an uninvited visitor, despite its links to the past of the characters or the community in which the protagonist lives. There is *excess* in horror's ghosts, monsters, apparitions, or possessions (i.e., their appearance, their ambiguity, the way they persist, their resistance to rational or natural explanations). We believe this excess speaks to their belonging to the field of that which has been dissociated, defensively excluded, and unrecognized.

The acclaimed horror novelist Stephen King suggests, in fact, that horror is a genre essentially allegorical regarding that which can only be expressed through displacement:

> Let us, then, assume that the horror story is allegorical by its nature, that it is symbolic. Let us assume that it is talking to us, like a patient on the analyst's couch, about one thing while it means another
>
> (1981, p. 64)

Then he adds: "What is the ghost, after all, that it should frighten us so much, but our own face?" (1981, p. 285). And, a few pages later: "[…] I began to wonder if the haunted house could not be turned into a kind of symbol of unexpiated sin [from our perspective, an unresolved trauma]" (1981, p. 387).

We argue that much of horror narrative has been devoted to metaphorizing the re-emergence of unprocessed traumatic wounds. Stories of ghosts that insist on communicating (e.g., *The Others* [Amenábar, 2001]), undefined enemies that tirelessly follow the protagonist (e.g., *It Follows* [Mitchell, 2014]), monsters that penetrate the domestic space (e.g., *The Babadook* [Kent, 2014]), houses that unfold into a dark and twisted copy of their rooms and corridors (e.g., *Relic* [James, 2020]; *The Night House* [Bruckner, 2021]), hidden basements that demand to be reopened (e.g., *The Conjuring* [Wan, 2013]; *The Changeling* [Medak, 1980]), walls pierced by a presence that observes from the other side (e.g., *His House* [Weekes, 2020]), passages that allow access to an alternate reality where complicated grief awaits (e.g., *Talk to Me* [Philipou, D. & Philipou, M, 2022]), indecipherable messages written in the harvest (e.g., *Signs* [Shyamalan, 2002]), etc., are all preoccupied with *something that returns*, the metaphor of painful experiences that have been registered but not integrated.

In fact, horror may be the genre through which our culture represents this phenomenology of traumatic repetition in the most evident and powerful way. Even in films that do not center around previous trauma, horror always narrates the exposure of the protagonists to a potentially traumatizing experience, that is, to an unexpected and inexplicable event that shatters our most basic assumptions about the world, about others, and about ourselves.

Guillermo del Toro poignantly expresses these ideas in the monologue that opens his film *The Devil's Backbone* (2001):

> What is a ghost? A terrible event condemned to repeat itself over and over. A moment of pain, perhaps. Something dead which, for a moment, seems to be alive still. A feeling suspended in time. Like a blurred photograph. Like an insect trapped in amber.

Even if characters within horror often deny the relationship between the monster and their past, they at the same time sense that it has something to do with them, something to say about them. Their adventure often consists of re-appropriating a pain that they themselves or previous generations were unable to recognize and process; in short, of being able to say: *I am what haunts me* (Martínez-Biurrun & Pitillas, 2021).

A similar movement is described by many therapeutic processes in the field of psychoanalysis. Our work with patients to overcome dissociation (Bromberg, 2011) can be experienced as an invitation to look more directly at those aspects of their experience that were unformulated (Stern, 2013), defensively excluded (Bowlby, 1980), operating as an unmentalized *alien self* (Fonagy, Luyten, & Allison, 2019), pressing from within as negative introjects (Fairbairn, 1952) that, as long as they remain unintegrated, tend to be reenacted in our relational world (Gleiser, 2003; Pitillas, 2020; Wachtel, 2014), make us vulnerable to disorganization (Liotti, 2004; Gleiser, 2003; Pitillas, 2020; Wachtel, 2014), or become visible in the 'theatres' of the body and psychosomatic distress (McDougall, 1989).

A socio-cultural dimension runs through the phenomenology of trauma (see, for example, Herman, 2015), just as it does in horror films. Within them, the staging of trauma crucially involves the other characters, who are forced first to believe or not believe the main character's story (which sounds like madness), and, then, to flee for their lives or else take sides with the protagonist and compromise their integrity. This dimension also involves the viewer, by conveying a reflection on the link between overcoming subjective fears and interacting with the community. Many of these narratives, in fact, carry a more or less implicit critique of the way in which society itself is a creator or perpetuator of trauma, through testimonies of injustice and lack of support for victims, or the dynamics of indifference or stigmatization of victims: responses that, even if by omission, side with the aggressors (Herman, 2015).

This book

The aim of this book is to trace some of horror cinema's explorations of (post-) traumatic phenomenology, and to reflect on some potential uses of this genre and its manifestations within therapeutic processes. Our analysis is directed at horror fiction as a whole, but we have chosen to refer to films for the vast majority of the examples. Because of its nature as a visual and time-bound spectacle, the structures and symbols employed in cinematic narrative tend to be sharper and more easily identifiable.

Our analogy between the psychology of trauma and the horror genre is based on a second premise, which adds to the one just stated. There is a special connection between the horror story and the way in which dream material (especially nightmares) is organized, the laws of primary processing, and the way in which dissociated traumatic contents re-emerge (when they do). Put more simply: horror cinema speaks a language similar to that of our unconscious mind (and, particularly, to that of the traumatized mind). In our view, this makes narrative horror the best cultural vehicle at our disposal for objectifying, naming, and narrating the elusive shadows that lurk in our unconscious.

This book consists of five chapters. The first three explore essential aspects of traumatic phenomenology that have been represented in complex and rich ways within contemporary cinematic horror.

In the first chapter, we describe *trauma as disruption*, that is, an experience that frontally shocks our maps of the world, shatters some of the basic assumptions that underpin our sense of self, agency and confidence, and involves an excess of stimulation or 'free energy' that resists processing. As a result, trauma tends to register anomalously, in the form of dissociated material, isolated from other contents of identity and, consequently, retaining its original emotional energy and its capacity to hurt the individual. In this chapter we explore the various ways in which the horror genre has shed light on this disruptive dimension of trauma.

In the second chapter, we describe *trauma as fragmentation*, that is, as the result of processes that force the mind to operate in a non-integrated way. The need to maintain a psychic balance, to keep some unbearable feelings at bay, to isolate ideas and thoughts that were not processed in time, etc., makes the traumatized mind a fragmentary mind. In this chapter, we explore the various ways in which the horror genre has shed light on this dimension of trauma.

In the third chapter, we describe *trauma as re-emergence*, that is, as the recurrence of emotions, ideas, memories, or interactive patterns that expose people to new experiences of pain or to a reinforcement of the traumatic experience. In this chapter, we explore the various ways in which the horror genre has shed light on this repetitive or cyclical dimension of trauma.

In the fourth chapter, we use narrative studies, anthropology, and cultural theory to trace the path taken by many characters in modern horror films, from the denial or rationalization of the threat to the defeat of the monster (or the final destruction of characters), through the recognition of the supernatural, the search for a mediation that helps to understand and confront the threat, or the character's self-surrender as a condition for salvation. Analogous to the Campbellian hero's journey – although with some relevant differences – this path includes a series of phases and the opportunity (not always fulfilled) for a climax that represents the integration of that which was previously hidden or unrecognized, that is, the integration of the trauma.

In the fifth chapter, we explore the potential therapeutic power of images, narratives, and horror metaphors in clinical work with traumatized patients. The chapter offers a preliminary model that considers the transitional nature of horror tropes, their ability to provide patients and therapists with symbolic means for expressing unprocessed aspects of trauma, and applications of the horror language to support parts of the (otherwise difficult) therapeutic dialogue with individuals suffering from traumatic histories.

Chapter 1

Traumatic disruption in modern horror cinema

Trauma results from one or more events that assault the subject and which are outside the order of the everyday and expected. These events always involve violence of some kind and, like any experience we face, demand psychic processing (Ogden et al., 2006).

However, some experiences go beyond what we are able to take in. Abuse at the hands of our peers, violent or unexpected loss, betrayal or unexpected abandonment of loved ones, torture, serious accidents, and natural disasters or war, among other experiences, can defy our usual operations of psychic metabolization and resist entering the register of the symbolic and being named (Boulanger, 2011; Caruth, 2013). They bring with them such novel stimulation that our predictive models of the world are overwhelmed, and the brain struggles to infer meaning from the experience or to predict what will come next (Kube et al., 2020). Asymmetries in the activation of different areas of the brain prevent integrated processing of what is happening (van der Kolk, 2015). Assumptions that underpin our basic trust in the world are revealed as insufficient or false (Janoff-Bulman, 1992). The absence of a supportive response from the environment or help in emotional processing can exacerbate the victim's negative feelings about themself, their doubts about the legitimacy of their pain, or their isolation (Benjamin, 2017; Herman, 2015).

Cathy Caruth suggests that "[…] the most direct seeing of a violent event may occur as an absolute inability to know it" (Caruth, 1996/2013, p. 92), and adds that, by subtracting itself from the associative circuit with which we assimilate the rest of our experiences, it remains in a status of un-constituted experience: "The shock of the mind's relation to the threat of death is thus not the direct experience of the threat, but precisely the missing of this experience, the fact that, not being experienced in time, it has not yet been fully known" (p.62). This is reminiscent of Stolorow and Atwood's considerations of an 'invalidated unconscious' that contains experiences that have not been articulated because they never evoked a response from the environment (1992). Thus, trauma functions as an unreadable experience, something that resists interpretation and rational ordering. The individual does not understand it, know how to respond, how to regulate the intensity of pain and fear that it provokes. Trauma, in short, drags us into the realm of 'meaninglessness.'

Many of the stories that make up the horror canon also seem to lean towards meaninglessness. Supernatural apparitions, monsters of incomprehensible shape or behavior, voices echoing across an empty house, and the dead coming back to haunt the living are some of its essential tropes, all pertaining to that which cannot be interpreted by reason and science. This parallelism of trauma in the realm of fantasy narratives would be what David Roas defines as "metaphysical fear," a sense of terror derived not so much from fright or a threat to physical integrity, but from the fact that 'our convictions about what is real cease to function, when we lose our footing in the face of a world that was once familiar to us' (2016, p. 96).

Trauma as a disruption of basic trust

In the early 1990s, Ronnie Jannoff-Bulman equated trauma with a "shattering" of the basic assumptions on which the self is based. We live under the assumption that there is a proportional, cause-effect relationship between what people do and the consequences of their actions. We assume that misfortune usually happens to other people. We trust that the future will be good to us (or, at least, fair). We believe that others (our most direct significant others, but also society and culture) have essentially good intentions, and that a moral code regulates human relationships. We assume that those who play protective roles in our lives will be reliable. We believe in the consistency and continuity of who we are. We believe in political systems as positive tools of social organization. We also believe that the cosmos, however large, operates according to laws that we can understand.

For Janoff-Bulman, these assumptions form a pre-conscious conceptual system that colors people's experiences and organizes their everyday behavior. These existential axioms are highly resistant to change, insofar as they provide us with the basic security that allows us to be in the world.

Participating in all these assumptions would guarantee a Winnicottian sense of 'going on being', an experience of continuity originally provided by a mother who is able to keep the baby protected from excessively intense emotions or extreme states of pain, hunger, excitement, etc. The presence of sensitive maternal care provides the infant with the essential belief that the world is a kind and trustworthy place. This constitutes something of a backdrop, an implicit background of security that underpins our everyday actions and interactions. In adulthood, new layers of confidence are added to the base of security built within the primary attachment relationship. These layers of trust stem from a shared identity and rituals within large groups (Volkan, 2018), among other sources.

That is, until a trauma takes place. Then:

> The assault on fundamental assumptions is massive. These traumatic events do not produce the psychological equivalent of superficial scratches that heal quickly, but deep wounds […] that require much more restorative efforts. What has been wounded is the victim's internal world.
>
> (Janoff-Bulman, 1992, p. 53)

With trauma, the individual is deprived of their previous knowledge systems; their core assumptions are fractured. "Traumatic events call into question basic human relationships," adds Herman, who further argues that these experiences:

> breach the attachments of family, friendship, love, and community. They shatter the construction of the self that is formed and sustained in relation to others. They undermine the belief system that gives meaning to human experience. They violate the victim's faith in a natural or divine order and cast the victim into a state of existential crisis.
>
> (2015, p. 51)

Three traumatic fractures in horror narrative

A large part of the horror narrative consists, essentially, of the metaphorized account of a traumatic experience, its consequences and manifestations. In horror films, the trauma may be an event from the past that threatens and invades the experience of the present (think, for example, of ghost stories). At other times, trauma takes place in the present, and massively questions the safety and structures that – we believe – keep us protected (consider any apocalyptic story or any story based on the threat of disasters, animals, or other adversaries that proliferate massively and threaten the structures of the world as we know it) (Derry, 2009).

The shattering of world maps and assumptions of safety that comes with trauma is, in a sense, a collapse of the symbolic authority that sustains our sense of who we are as individuals and societies. This breakdown of authority has a powerful correlate in many horror films where the characters discover, to their despair, that referential figures of safety (the sheriff, the father, the doctor) are unable to perceive, diagnose, or respond to the supernatural threat that haunts them. In Chapter 4 we will explore in more detail how these elements are arranged in the narrative structures of the genre. Suffice it to say that one of the tropes of horror fiction is precisely the uselessness of codes, uniforms, and symbols previously associated with knowledge and protection. In horror cinema, the maps of the world are blurred.

Perhaps the traumatic disruptions that horror fiction has most frequently explored are those that affect three basic human assumptions: self/body, other, and world.

The self and the body

Our psychic life is sustained by the assumption that a cohesive, coherent, and continuous self defines us across change and the passage of time, and that this self is ourselves. The fantasy of the self also includes the notion that the contents of our inner world are accessible to consciousness. Memories, feelings, aspirations, fantasies, etc., are the property of an individual who has mastery over their inner world. We are convinced that we can know ourselves. Finally, we are confident that these contents of our mind are essentially good and acceptable.

Horror fiction thrives on stories in which the character is confronted with events that collide head-on with these basic assumptions. Many of these characters are drawn into 'adventures' that force them to confront an unrecognizable, dark version of themselves.

Narratives centered on the figure of the 'double,' for example, directly challenge the notion of a self-contained self. The concept of the double, or 'doppelgänger,' in contemporary horror cinema and narrative draws heavily from Freud's notion of the uncanny ("*das unheimliche*" [S. Freud, 1919/1945]), which explores the eerie and unsettling feeling when something familiar is rendered strange. In horror, the double often manifests as an alter ego, twin, or shadow self, embodying repressed fears, desires, and aspects of identity that challenge the protagonist's sense of self. This theme capitalizes on the intrinsic human fear of losing control or encountering a mirrored version of oneself that harbors malevolent intentions. Such representations invoke existential dread, questioning the stability of personal identity and highlighting the potential for evil within the self.

Contemporary horror narratives utilize the double to explore complex psychological themes and societal anxieties. Films like Jordan Peele's *Us* (2019) and Darren Aronofsky's *Black Swan* (2010) exemplify this by depicting characters confronted with sinister doubles that reveal hidden facets of their psyche or societal inequalities. The double serves as a narrative device to externalize internal conflicts, making abstract fears tangible and visually impactful. This not only intensifies the horror experience but also allows for a deeper exploration of themes such as duality, madness, and the human capacity for violence and self-destruction. Through the lens of the double, contemporary horror delves into the shadows of the human mind, unearthing the uncanny within the familiar.

Perhaps this model was inaugurated in the horror canon with *The Strange Case of Dr Jekyll and Mr Hyde*, a novel by Robert Louis Stevenson published in 1886. The scientist protagonist, in his attempt to separate the good aspects from the evil aspects of human nature, creates a substance that, every night, transforms him into the worst version of himself: Mr Hyde. Hyde is a man that gives in to his drives, is aggressive, indifferent to law and order, and homicidal. An interesting point in this novel, often overlooked, is that Jekyll, having experienced the effects of his potion once or twice, becomes addicted to its use: the emergence of his most bestial self provides a catharsis that he finds hard to relinquish and which will ultimately be the cause of his self-destruction.

A century later, we find *The Dark Half* (Stephen King's 1989 novel, adapted to film by George A. Romero in 1993) which presents a variation on Jekyll and Hyde in which an author named Thad Beaumont is forced to 'kill' the pseudonym under which he wrote his most violent and successful novels, George Stark. The non-existent dead man then escapes from his grave of props, acquiring corporeality for the first time, and goes on a murderous rampage, creating an encirclement of suspicion around Beaumont – since they share fingerprints, despite their contrasting physical appearance – with the aim of forcing him to write a new novel attributed to Stark. As with Jekyll's addiction, Beaumont also takes undisguised pleasure – his wife is a witness – whenever he assumes the persona of his alias in order to write. Stark represents the violent impulses and the yearning for unbridled masculinity that must be repressed in order to be a good husband and father, so it is impossible for Beaumont to regard Stark as alien to his own personality. Indeed, the fact that the police's suspicions about the murders fall on him functions as more than a mere tool of suspense, and takes on a symbolic character: it makes sense to suspect the protagonist, because he himself would have wished to carry out these murders (Stark is, after all, a materialization of the darker parts of himself, as the title implies).

Enemy (2013), Denis Villeneuve's film based on José Saramago's 2002 novel *The Double* (*O Homem Duplicado*), works in a similar way. It begins with the enigmatic phrase: "Chaos is order as yet undeciphered" and presents a passive university professor with grey routines who by chance discovers the existence of a film actor with exactly the same physique. The actor represents, in addition to the extroversion and audacity that the professor lacks, the dream of breaking with routine and escaping the prison of an ordinary life (encouraged, moreover, by a mother figure that Villeneuve symbolizes visually in a colossal spider with resonances to the sculptures of Louise Bourgeois). As in so many other films concerned with the double, the protagonist's initial fascination with this reflection of himself eventually leads to a destructive ending, in which one of the two versions is sacrificed.

These stories (and their common outcome: the death of one of the two halves) reflect a finding familiar to psychoanalysis: we are not prepared to acknowledge, on an ongoing basis, the less civilized, more primal areas of our psyche. That other half, the alligators that according to Stephen King dwell in the basement of our minds (1981), are the raw material of many horror stories.

The tension between diverse – and often opposing – identities within a person is another trope of horror fiction. From *Psycho* (Hitchcock, 1960), in which Norman Bates' desires struggle against the demands of the controlling, homicidal mother within his mind, to *Split* (Shyamalan, 2016), in which the protagonist takes into his mind the identities of his childhood abuser, the child he himself was, and the demanding mother or the avenger, among others, many horror films have looked at the fragmentation of the self. For these stories, identity is a fragile, permeable construction.

There is a strong parallel between this type of narration and one of the important features of post-traumatic psychology. After being exposed to the impact of trauma (especially if it is interpersonal in nature), the self can be 'inhabited' by an alien voice: that of the perpetrator. In health, our mind is the stage for a multiplicity of voices from our social experience: our parents, teachers, friends and partners often – and without our being fully aware of it – resonate inside our head, they are commentators on what is happening to us, an internal audience where diversity and integration combine: we live adaptively in the spaces between these dissociated versions of ourselves (Bromberg, 1998). This natural multiplicity of the self can be pushed to extreme levels under conditions of trauma and take the form of 'haunting:' the voices that are heard inside the mind are not the property of the individual, but negative presences that penetrate subjectivity and actualize the horror that was experienced in the past. During trauma, the victim is not only stripped of all power and subjected to a situation of violence or exploitation; they also become captive to the voice of the aggressor (Ferenczi, 1933; Frankel, 2002). The aggressor's contempt and hatred are introjected by a mind that is profoundly helpless. This identification with the aggressor is the desperate operation of a psyche which, exposed to violence from which it is impossible to escape, ends up taking on the aggressor's perspective on the self: *you are despicable, you are filthy, you deserve to be harmed* (a more detailed development of this theme is presented in Chapter 2).

A variation of the belief in the self is the assumption of the integrity of the body, the consistency of its boundaries, and its accessibility to our will. Trauma exposes us to the realization that we actually inhabit an organism that is fragile, and over which we have very little control. According to Dent, when we are exposed to overwhelming pain or threat, our physiology can be altered in radical ways, abruptly removing us from our previous experience of *having* a body (2020). The body organizes itself around a readiness for danger, which disturbs (sometimes chronically) the nervous, endocrine, immune, and other systems. Hyperactivation of the sympathetic nervous system, suspension or disruption of other metabolic functions, decreased immune efficiency, abrupt oscillations between states of alter and states of dissociative dullness, increased (or, in the long term, decreased and flattened) cortisol, etc., are some of the ways in which a traumatized body transforms its policies. These imbalances can, in turn, destabilize essential psychological functions such as memory, impulse control, emotional regulation, mentalization, etc. (Dent, 2020).

Under abuse, torture, or rape, people may lose control over bodily functions, sensitivity in certain areas, or their physiological responses.[1] The victim goes from having a 'subjectified' body (imbued with the individual's will and desires) to having an 'objectified' body, a *thing* that can be controlled, penetrated, damaged by others. The experience of mind-body continuity that we usually take for granted is thus reduced.

In many cases, horror fiction treats the body as a surface that, contrary to our beliefs, we do not fully understand or control. It is full of bodies inhabited or assaulted by something that the subject does not recognize or master; of masks or voices that convey the presence of 'something else'; of hands that obey a will alien to that of the protagonist; etc. For these stories, the body is not the seat of a free and conscious subjectivity, but an 'alien' place, a 'heterotopia' (Foucault, 2008/1967).

This impression that our body is not our own is particularly accentuated in 'body horror,' whose most famous representative may be the Canadian director, David Cronenberg. The protagonists of his stories often discover that their bodies are subject to pathologies and metamorphoses stemming from an emotional or instinctual excess. In Cronenberg's films, the boundaries between psyche and soma are blurred. Hatred, sexual arousal, or unresolved traumas materialize in the form of excrescences, pustules, or anatomical alterations that provoke dread and blur the boundaries of the skin.

The clearest version of these ideas can be found in *The Brood* (Cronenberg, 1979). In this film, Dr. Hal Raglan, through his 'psychoplasmatic' method, manages

Figure 1.1 In *The Brood* (Cronenberg, 1979), Nola's psychic pain emerges in the form of bodily transformations, particularly a strange baby, born of out Nola's post-traumatic rage.

to make trauma-related emotions emerge in the form of strange bodily marks. This facilitates a kind of physical catharsis that frees people from the emotional weight associated with their traumas. The method, however, has an uncontrolled effect on one of the patients, Nola Carveth. As a child, Nola was physically and verbally abused by her alcoholic mother and abandoned by her father. Nola's devastating emotions manifest outwardly in the form of strange creatures that 'come out' of her to execute some of the people in Nola's life (her own mother and daughter among them). In one of the film's climactic scenes, Nola lifts up her dress to reveal a set of excrescences growing on her torso. The largest of these is a strange baby, born of Nola's trauma and perhaps a future avenger of the wrongs she has suffered.

These considerations bring us back to what is perhaps one of the most difficult realizations to process: we inhabit a corruptible and mortal flesh. There is a kind of horror that reminds us of just that: we are nothing more than an accumulation of muscle, fat, and brain, no different from the beef and pork we eat every day in neatly sliced and packaged portions. Such is the simple and maddening message conveyed by *The Texas Chainsaw Massacre*, a belief that Leatherface's family follows through to its ultimate end, much to the dismay of the group of young people who cross their path (Hooper, 1974).

This 1974 film and others like it (for example, Wes Craven's *The Last House on the Left,* made two years earlier) appear in a historical period in which American society was coping with the trauma of the Vietnam War, which involved the repetitive viewing of American soldiers killed by the thousands in a war that, as the years went by, made less sense. The massive and illogical death, and the uninterrupted return of young corpses to their families, brought with it the shocking realization of our fragile carnality. These films' detailed scenes of subjugation and torture seem to be a cultural reenactment of America's collective trauma. In them, the bodies are seen (and used) by the aggressor in their purest physicality.

Finally, the horror narrative challenges our well-established notion that our self is the seat of essentially acceptable tendencies and emotions. Both at the individual level and at the level of collective psychology (Volkan, 2018), a basic projective mechanism operates, whereby we place ugliness, envy, and aggression in the Other. Horror narrative, however, takes away this fantasy that the monstrous is outside of us. In the words of Linda Holland-Toll: "Placing the monster within the human body rejects the argument of evil as something located in the other" (2001, p. 3).

Perhaps this idea underlies some of the fiction about demonic possession. The plot that moves these stories on a superficial level (the struggle between Good and Evil, or God vs Satan) seem also to question those very boundaries that place goodness on the inside in order to relegate evil to the outside. Subjectivity ceases to be clearly delimited and protected from the dark, which – as we discover – can also be part of oneself. The terror of the demonic deconstructs traditional assumptions of the moral cleansing of the self (note that the victim of possession is often a figure traditionally clothed in purity, such as a child, or a mother), and, again, shows how our bodies and our subjectivities can be the realm of destructive drives. Even when the monster is presented as an absolute Other, alien to the body and even to the nature of the protagonist, in the end it will reveal itself symbolically as a mirror image.

Others and relationships

The background of security that we need in order to live is supported both by the perceived continuity of the self and by the perception that others are also consistent and legible. Moreover, we live in the belief that those who make up our closest network of relationships are on our side, harboring benevolent intentions towards us. This translates into a basic assumption: relationships are sources of protection, exchange, growth. The bonds of romance, friendship, or between parents and children, are foundational pillars of trust.

The horror narrative mocks – like many traumas do – this basic human belief, questioning its validity or even transforming it into a nightmare. Films such as *Invasion of the Body Snatchers* (Kaufman, 1978), *The Thing* (Carpenter, 1982), *Species* (Donaldson, 1995), or *Under the Skin* (Glazer, 2013), present us with stories where people are supplanted by alien creatures that take on their appearance. The world of recognizable bodies and faces (partners, lovers, relatives) becomes a façade that hides destructive creatures, eager to invade the protagonist and steal their identity, as they have done with others.

The nightmare of losing interpersonal references and of the most intimate other becoming an aggressor is also what defines many of the traumas that occur in the sphere of family intimacy. Victims of gender-based violence, child abuse, sexual abuse, betrayal, or abandonment suffer not only from the aggression they have received, but especially from what D.N. Stern describes as an "intersubjective disorientation" (2005): *Who is the other? Who am I to him? How am I seen by the one who attacks me? Why does he do it?* Trauma brings these questions to the fore and reveals them as the site of a void: in reality, we cannot really know *who* (in horror fiction: *what*) is hiding behind the face of the other.

Perhaps the negative transformation of the other can reach its most terrifying heights within the framework of parent–child attachment relationships. In some myths and fairy tales, the mother, giver of life and protector of the child, can be transformed into a devouring and persecutory creature, perhaps as an expression of one of our most atavistic fears: that of being dependent on parents who, in addition to caring, can control and harm us. The aggressive, dissociated, affectively disturbed face of a parent is an incomprehensible and terrifying stimulus for a young child (see Beebe & Lachman, 2014; Lyons-Ruth, Bronfman, & Parsons, 1999), whose psychological survival depends precisely on the love of their caregivers. The child finds themself in a kind of interpersonal impasse: the parents are a source of threat and pain and, at the same time, the only possible salvation from it (Johnston & Boyle, 2018; Main & Solomon, 1990). Under these conditions, for the child, the social world becomes a scene of terror.

Cinema has echoed this basic anthropological nightmare through films of a subgenre that Sarah Arnold (2016) describes as "maternal horror." In *Carrie*, we follow the story of a teenage girl raised by a single mother with a conservative and rigid religiosity (De Palma, 1976). The mother vigilantly monitors and severely punishes any signs of Carrie's autonomy, sexuality, or maturity (even when these signs are involuntary and beyond Carrie's control, such as when she experiences her first menstruation). Something similar happens in *Psycho*, where Norman Bates lives under the almost omnipotent control of a mother determined to destroy young women, potential rivals with whom Norman might fall in love (Hitchcock, 1960). These mothers in film actively fight against their offspring's attempts at differentiation. They also try to override their children's sexuality and, when it emerges irremediably, they seek to destroy it. Often, the supernatural threats of these fictions are a symbolic expression of the terrible mother's attempts to dominate or punish, and of the child's impulse to save themselves from or punish this mother. The aggressive birds in the eponymous film could be interpreted as the expression of the competitive impulse of a mother who resists being displaced by her son's new girlfriend (Hitchcock, 1963). The young Carrie's destructive, telekinetic abilities function as an outlet for Carrie's unspoken pain and hatred of her mother (and, alternatively, of a society and peers that harm her).

We find another variation on the mother-monster theme in *The Babadook* (Kent, 2014). Here, the conflict is not so much based on the mother's desires for control or fusion, but rather on the fact that the mother, as a consequence of her own trauma (the loss of her husband on the same day she gave birth to her child), sees her love

Figure 1.2 *The Babadook* (Jennifer Kent, 2014) depicts the traumatic transformation of a nurturing, protecting figure into a monstrous source of threat.

for the child transformed into hatred and rejection. The monster that attacks the nuclear family in this film may represent (among other things) the mother's feelings of rejection towards a child whom she irrationally holds responsible for her widowhood.

The sinister transformation of a nurturing space into a terrifying space may also be the result of the intergenerational transmission of trauma: the unresolved wounds of one generation (the parents) impact, in often unforeseen or unrecognized ways, on the next generation (the children). The contamination of parent–child relationships by trauma from previous generations has been the subject of films such as *Dark Water* (Nakata, 2002), *Color Out of Space* (Stanley, 2019), *Run* (Chaganty, 2020), *Hereditary* (Aster, 2018), and others (these issues are developed in detail in Chapter 3).

The world or cosmos

Our ability to move through and relate to our environment depends on another basic assumption: the world is as we perceive it. A corollary to this axiom is the belief that the world lends itself to our scientific understanding and technical control: a world that is tailored to our perception is a world that can be conquered, manipulated. Traumatic experiences linked to accidents and natural disasters challenge these axiomatic beliefs, confronting us with the unforgiving nature of an environment that is disproportionately large and hostile. Films about earthquakes, tornadoes, volcanoes, and other variations on the end of the world have appealed to the sensitivity our brains have acquired, over thousands of years of evolution, to the vast and adverse environments in which our species evolved.

Derry refers to this subgenre as "Horror of Armageddon," and states that one of its forms consists of the presentation of a world that is "constantly being threatened with extinction, usually by nonhuman, unindividualized creatures such as birds, bats, bees, frogs, snakes, rabbits, ants, or plants" (2009, p. 56), in what seem like cinematic variations on biblical accounts of divine punishment. The frightening thing about these narratives, Derry tells us, is precisely the absence of a transcendental logic or moral plan that we can decipher and make sense of. In these films, the world is presented to us as a mechanical and indifferent adversary, making the situation genuinely terrifying. In the face of these entities, our vulnerability is presented in its most naked expression; it becomes clear that we are small in the cosmos. In reference to *The Thing from Another World* (Christian Nyby, 1951) – the first adaptation of John W. Campbell's 1938 story *Who Goes There?*, later adapted by John Carpenter in *The Thing* (1982) – the external aggressor "does not violate our civilization's rules of conduct or the universe's natural order; it merely conducts itself independently of these things and therein lies the horror" (Derry, 2009, p. 57).

These threats are indifferent to our condition, our representations of the world and civilization, and, of course, to our desires. They do not participate in our cultural or moral sensibilities. We find these narrative developments in novels such as John Wyndham's *Day of the Triffids* (1951), Stephen King's *The Stand* (1978), and in much of the 'zombie' fiction that grew out of George A. Romero's foundational film *Night of the Living Dead* (1968).

The adversaries of this subgenre may also be endowed with an 'eerie' quality, something Mark Fisher defines as the impression produced when, where there should be nothing, there *is* something (2016). In *The Birds*, for example, we are terrified – we find it eerie – to witness how these winged creatures, hitherto driven by simple instinctive mechanisms, now seem to be directed and organized by some kind of purposeful intelligence, some kind of plan (Hitchcock, 1963). Suddenly, there is *something* – the intelligence, the plan – where there should be *nothing*. We feel the eerie when we are confronted with the manifestation of an external agent that arranges or moves things in reality according to a logic that is inaccessible to us (the author gives as examples the impression we get when we contemplate places like Stonehenge or the sculptures on Easter Island, settings created by cultures and codes that escape our current understanding). It is clear that the birds attack because they have set out to do so, but *what* exactly have they set out to do? They attack in an intelligent and deliberate way, but *who* or what has provided them with intelligence? What is the agent of this change? They are strongly motivated to harm us, but why? What do they want? What do they think? What do they feel – for it is also evident that some feeling, which should not exist, but does exist, moves the birds? Where we should only find pure animal automatism, we find a determination that is destructive and, worse, unintelligible to its victims. With the horrifying, the fabric of representations with which we cover and sustain our reality is torn apart, our compass of the world is unsettled. Horror fiction, again, fractures our basic assumptions.

This nightmare of a hostile or inscrutable world finds its most popular expression in cosmic horror, whose stories often present us with relatively everyday settings (the village, the farm by the woods, the house) where strange manifestations occur that do not easily lend themselves to scientific explanation. In *Color Out of Space* (Stanley, 2019), based on a story of the same name by Lovecraft (1927), a family who have moved to the countryside to get away from the memory of various traumas are confronted with the consequences of a meteorite crashing on their land. From the crater caused by the meteorite emerges an unclassifiable color, not belonging to the chromatic spectrum of our world, as well as a foul smell that cannot be defined either. The threat comes from a section of the Universe that does not correspond to our own, and so the color that fell from space is an alien color, genuinely *other*. This confronts the characters – and the spectator – with the possibility of inhabiting a Universe that transcends our perception and comprehension capacities, as well as being hostile.

It is a trope that runs through much of Lovecraftian and other contemporary cosmic horror productions. Simple geometry can also be traumatic because of its scale – as in the case of Lovecraft's own 'obscene' architectures – or because of its form. In Junji Ito's manga *Uzumaki*, a small Japanese village is invaded by the symbol of the spiral, which manifests itself in monstrous ways in the most unexpected places, to the point of driving everyone to obsession and madness. As Eugene Thacker argues, in Ito's comic:

> the spiral is more than just a mere pattern in nature; it is also equivalent to the very *idea* of the spiral itself [...] [The spiral] is ultimately equivalent to thought itself, understood here not simply as the private, individual thoughts of a person. The spiral-as-thought is 'thought' as the inhuman, 'thought' as equivalent to the world-without-us.
>
> (2011, p. 110)

Unpeeling, awakening, dis/ease

The impacts of trauma on our maps of the world (relating to self, other, and cosmos) contribute to what in horror fiction manifests as a progressive *'unpeeling'* of reality. Our shared knowledge of the world, which underpins our identity and our social transactions, is revealed as little more than a comfortable fiction. John Clute, who coined the term, says about unpeeling something that could well be said about psychic trauma:

> There is a gradual erasure of the paths on the world map [and] everything is false [...] The phenomenal world is revealed as a crust that, once removed, exposes the voids within the false consciousness of 'normal life' and the imposture of world history, a history we have been taught to understand as a narrative that justifies our lives [...].
>
> (2006, pp. 47–48)

For Clute, the world we think we possess is, in reality, a world that holds us *captive*. This is reminiscent of a central aspect of traumatic experience: an impression of smallness and helplessness. As Janoff-Bulman suggests, trauma strips us of that set of shared representations that, beneath the surface, hide chaos or emptiness (1992). Horror fiction, as a "narrative of awakening" (so named by Stuart Hanscomb [2010]), immerses us in this lucid nightmare: "Horror is that category of stories set in worlds that are false until the tale is told" (Clute, 2006).

Clute's unpeeling effect parallels what Holland-Toll (2001) has called dis/ease, meaning the realization that, behind the veils of society and culture, human relations are made up of aggressive or perverse logics: we are together as a society at the expense of others being excluded; to feel valuable and good, we project our sense of inferiority or ugliness onto others; although we describe our social bonds in terms of cooperation, love, and respect, undercurrents of control, threat, hatred, or fear of the other are at play beneath the surface. This realization, Holland-Toll argues, cannot be reduced or shut down by strategies of reason or by recourse to the cohesive logics of community. Dis/ease drags us into the realm of "radical doubt" and "anti-closure." For the author, the purpose of horror is precisely to "redefine and reorder the social landscape," "subvert commonly accepted cultural models," or "tear the veil" (an expression originally used by Clive Barker (Badley, 1996).

Holland-Toll is particularly interested in a dis/ease concerning American (by extension, First World) community life, where apparent social harmony often conceals dynamics of exclusion, stigmatization, scapegoating, and so on. Some horror fictions reveal to us that these negative logics are precisely the basis on which the social is constituted (a notion brilliantly represented by David Lynch in the sequence that opens *Blue Velvet* [1986], where we discover that the ground on which the inhabitants of the idyllic town of Lumberton walk is infested by a microscopic chaos of insects that kill and eat each other).

In Shirley Jackson's famous story *The Lottery*, we are shown how community life in a small American town is nourished each year by the ritual stoning of one of its citizens (1948). More recently, Jordan Peele explored another dis/ease-based thesis in *Us* (2019). The film suggests that for every prosperous family, there is an underground copy composed of degraded versions of the 'original' family members. The members of these *doppelgänger* families are what we would see if we were to look into a distorting mirror: a deformed, primitive variation of each member of the 'real' family. The nightmare into which this film plunges us is – as is almost always the case in horror fiction – that of a return of the repressed: the dark counterpart of each family reappears at night, in front of the doors of their houses, ready to reconquer its place in the 'real' world, which is the one above.

A Nightmare on Elm Street also participates in this notion according to which an aberrant logic is hidden in the basement of community life (Craven, 1984). The nightmares that haunt and kill its young protagonists are the re-emergence of a vengeful being (Freddy Krueger) whom their parents executed, years ago, outside of the law. The neighborhood in which these young people live comfortably, with their modern cars, their stereos, and their teenage romances, is sustained by a crime (a trauma) that was repressed and now haunts the next generation.

Trauma as a disruption in the processing of experience

We have described trauma as an experience that impacts the psyche but is not processed by the psyche through its usual resources of processing and symbolization. Trauma is an attack on the symbolic order. The experience of traumatized people is that of an impossibility to *say*, with the shared codes of culture and language, what they have lived through. The network of words and representations that we share and use to account for reality proves useless when it comes to expressing the experience of those who have lost a loved one in difficult circumstances, those who have been victims of rape, those who have been forced to attack or kill others, and so on. Expressed in Lacanian terms, the traumatic involves the irruption of an excessive Real in people's lives. This Real is a surplus of stimulation, incomprehensible and inexpressible, which violently tears the fabric of the Symbolic and leaves us, literally, mute. Throughout this section we will detail some important aspects of this premise and address the ways in which horror cinema has explored this dimension of traumatic phenomenology.

Predictive processing and metaphor

As noted in the previous section, our minds make sense of ongoing experience by linking incoming stimulation to internal representational schemas that make sense of what is going on in the world around us. According to Modell, our psyche organizes the complexity of experience through present–past analogies, or what he calls "metaphorical" processing (1997; 2005; 2009). This prevents the events of our lives from being experienced as a source of novel and violent stimulation. We know where we are and what is happening through comparison with previous memories and meanings that provide a framework for interpreting the experience: *you are here, this is what is happening, this is you.* Metaphor allows us both to establish similarities between separate moments in our biography and to detect nuances and differences. By means of metaphor, we not only tie novelty to past experience so it acquires meaning, we also retroactively transform the meaning of our history in the light of what we experience in the present (see also D.B. Stern, 2012).

Trauma clashes against the metaphorical, dynamic character of our memory. The impact, so radically unexpected and painful, does not serve as a metaphor for anything we have experienced or are able to remember (Modell, 2005). Traumatic memories, encapsulated and separated from the web of content that shapes our identity, resist change. The creative tension between who we were and who we are is interrupted; the opportunity to draw similarities and make comparisons is lost, and the trauma retains its original state.

Along a similar line, the Predictive Processing Framework (PPF) suggests that the human brain continuously compares incoming sensory input with its internal predictive models of the world. This constant comparison aims to minimize prediction error, i.e., the discrepancy between expected and actual sensory input. The brain uses past experiences and prior knowledge ('priors') to anticipate and interpret the environment efficiently and maximize adaptation (A. Clark, 2013; Friston, 2010).

Psychological trauma introduces a significant amount of volatility into this system. Due to their intensity and emotional charge, traumatic experiences cause drastic disruptions in the brain's predictive models. These disturbing events are often so extreme and alien to the individual's prior experiences that existing priors become insufficient to predict and manage future situations (van der Kolk, 2015). This results in an overload of prediction error, leaving the brain in a constant state of uncertainty and hyper-alertness (Hohwy, 2013).

The inability of predictive models to adequately adapt to new traumatic information leads to a perpetual cycle of predictive mismatch. The brain struggles to reconcile expectations with the lived experience, something that can manifest as disproportionate responses to stimuli reminiscent of the traumatic event, generating hypervigilance, anxiety, and other stress-related symptoms (Courtois & Ford, 2009). This persistent mismatch and resulting volatility not only affect the individual's emotional well-being but can also impair daily functioning.

Two characteristics of traumatic experiences contribute in particular to this failure of processing, this suspension of metaphor in the context of traumatic impacts: 'freezing' and 'silencing.' The experience of the victim during the unfolding of the trauma is that of being helpless in the face of something that happens to them, unable to move (freezing) and unable to protest or ask for help (silencing).

Freeze to survive

The inability to move is a central feature of trauma. During events of high-emotional impact, when pain and fear reach very intense levels, and escape is impossible, our psyche tends to become paralyzed and disconnected. Polyvagal theory suggests that sensory or emotional disconnection, freezing, and behavioral paralysis are manifestations of dorsal vagus nerve activity. When this pathway is activated, organisms may freeze or feign death to avoid predators, conserve energy during healing, or adopt submissive attitudes to reduce external aggression (Hill, 2015). Extreme hypoactive states are a kind of 'blackout' that our organism resorts to when it is helpless (unable to save itself or call for help) in the face of threat. Like an overloaded electrical system, the organism chooses to switch off, it takes an escape when there is no escape.

Freezing is a strategy for surviving inescapable fear or pain, but, in turn, it blocks the reactions and movements that the organism would need to carry out in the face of the threat (such as screaming, running, hitting, shaking, etc.). As we will see in later sections, overcoming post-traumatic events necessarily involves the recovery of a basic mobility of the body that was – and remains – frozen. This concept is supported by various scientific and therapeutic approaches. 'Somatic experiencing,' developed by Peter Levine, emphasizes the importance of physical movement in trauma recovery, highlighting that trauma induces a physiological state of immobility or 'freezing' that can persist long after the traumatic event. Recovery involves re-establishing physical movement and allowing the body to complete the interrupted fight-or-flight response (Levine, 2010). Additionally, the freeze response is a well-documented reaction to trauma, where the body enters a state of immobility to protect itself. This response can become chronic if unresolved, leading to conditions such as post-traumatic stress disorder (PTSD). Re-engaging the body through movement and physical therapy can help "thaw" this state and support trauma recovery (Levine, 2010; van der Kolk, 2015). From a neuroscientific perspective, trauma impacts brain functioning, particularly the amygdala, hippocampus, and autonomic nervous system, resulting in a heightened state of alertness associated with physical symptoms of being 'stuck' or frozen. Recovery strategies involving physical activity can help reset these systems, promoting a return to normal physiological states and aiding overall healing (MacLean, 1990; van der Kolk, 2015).

In parallel, many horror films teach us that overcoming the supernatural threat requires the characters to regain some control over their bodies, which have been subdued or invaded by the threat. The active, face-to-face confrontation with the monster, the execution of an extreme movement that releases pain or contained impulses (see, for example, the classic scene of Isabelle Adjani's crazed dance in *Possession* [Zulawski, 1981]), or the initiation of an escape response, among others, constitute forms of final overcoming of traumatic paralysis in a significant number of horror films. We find a recent example in *Midsommar*, where the protagonist, unable to resolve her grief over the violent death of her family and to get out of a destructive romantic relationship, manages to move towards healing thanks to the help of the Harga women, who cry and scream when she cannot (Aster, 2019). Later, Dani is able to take a further step towards unfreezing thanks to a hallucinatory dance she performs with these women, under the effect of a psychoactive substance. This step brings her closer to the core of the violent ritual practiced among the Harga, which includes the suicide of members of the community, or the torture and sacrifice of outsiders. Thus, what began as a sequence of movements offering the protagonist the opportunity to thaw emotionally and regain her will within a community that lends her a voice, from the midpoint of the film leans towards the side of revenge, and the pathological 'overcoming' of traumatic pain. The last step in Dani's perverse 'healing' involves a final active move: she gives up her partner in ritual sacrifice. Taken together, each of these scenes traces a path that, starting from the post-traumatic blockade, leads to a liberation of bodily and affective expressivity, a recovery of desire and psychic energy (albeit with very dark consequences) as an alternative way of living with the trauma.

Dissociation combines an experience of emotional emptiness (not feeling) and a behavioral state of passivity (submitting). Dissociative states function as a desperate survival strategy: for the child on the receiving end of the beating, for example, remaining silent and immobile decreases the likelihood that the adult will remain irritated or angry. Over many years of evolution, the most vulnerable individuals in human communities – children, women, prisoners – have known the protective potential of silence and passivity. But this is not exclusive to these groups; anyone is vulnerable to entering these states if they are immersed in an experience of unbearable pain while being helpless.

Under the effect of dissociation and paralysis, trauma is experienced as something that takes place 'out there', an event detached from the perceiving subject. Many victims report that, during the occurrence of their traumas, they were external witnesses to what was happening to them, they felt as if they were 'watching it on a television screen' or 'as if it were happening to someone else.'

The self-anesthesia involved in dissociative states compromises the processing and, in the long term, integration of traumatic experience. Perception is dulled and, although what is happening is happening to the person, they are 'expelled' from the scene. Their ability to process what is happening, to think or communicate the experience in words, is suspended. Our mind is not quite there to think and understand what is happening, and the contents of the trauma 'creep into' the psyche clandestinely.

Dissociation during trauma significantly increases the individual's vulnerability to developing chronic PTSD. Dissociation acts as a coping mechanism that allows individuals to detach from the unbearable aspects of the traumatic experience. While this mechanism may provide immediate relief, it interferes with the normal processing and integration of the traumatic memory, thereby increasing the risk of chronic PTSD (Briere, 2006; Lanius, Vermetten, & Pain, 2010).

Research indicates that dissociation involves disruptions in the integrated functions of consciousness, memory, identity, and perception of the self and the environment. These disruptions can lead to a chronic pattern of emotional and psychological distress. As already stated, individuals who dissociate during trauma are often unable to fully process the traumatic event, making them more susceptible to PTSD (Dell & O'Neil, 2009; Stein et al., 2013).

Dissociation also tends to generalize, leading to a recursive pattern of difficulties – a vicious circle. The more one dissociates, the more unmanageable the traumatic experience becomes, increasing the need to dissociate again during times of stress or when faced with post-traumatic reminders, as the organism enters states of alertness (Perry et al., 1995).

Roman Polanski's portrayal of a post-traumatic state in *Repulsion* (1965) is a good reference to these phenomena. Carol, a victim of childhood sexual abuse, frequently enters into daydreams and states of mental absence that her colleagues and clients in the beauty salon reproach her with: "Have you fallen asleep?" As the story progresses and Carol descends into a spiral of pain and psychic fragmentation, the gestures with which she tries to escape the experience and dissociate become more compulsive: she bites her nails, she chews her hair, she sings to herself in a childish, hypnotic tone, she scratches herself, she swings. As the film unravels, these mechanisms are not only insufficient, but also seem to render Carol even more vulnerable in the face of the impending re-emergence of traumatic memories and pain.

Silencing, shaming, and failure of recognition

Dissociative freezing is a phenomenon that takes place on an individual, intrapsychic level. But trauma does not only paralyze us from within. By silencing and disempowering victims, the environment can also contribute to the victims' inability to react, defend themselves, and talk about what has happened (Doka, 2017; Turner & Stauffer, 2023).

Many early traumas based on physical violence, for example, are built on a dangerous combination of adult aggression with narrative prohibition or the absence of a recognizing, regulating relational environment. Think, for example, of some of the prohibitions surrounding childhood sexual abuse: "This didn't happen, you probably dreamt or imagined it;" "if you tell, it will be worse;" "You mustn't talk about it, it's too painful;" "He would never do anything like that;" and so on. Disavowal of the victim's suffering – of this or other types of trauma – can take the form of a distorted sharing of responsibility ("you made me do this to you"); a denial of the violent nature of the act ("I did it to help you understand") or of its painful effects ("don't exaggerate," "it couldn't possibly have hurt you"); or the threat of increased levels of pain or isolation ("if you keep crying I'll give you something to complain about," "you're making me very nervous and I'm going to leave") (Sluzky, 2006). People in mourning, those who have suffered violence, migrants or war-displaced individuals, and soldiers returning from the front, among others, often share a sense that the world, in more or less subtle ways, expects them to pull themselves together and not make too much noise.

The repetition of these dynamics gives rise to significant narrative distortions that confuse the victim well into adulthood: *Did it really happen? Who did it? What did I feel? Did I provoke it? Why did it happen to me? What is it about me that has produced this?* Speaking about the trauma and giving it narrative order becomes increasingly difficult as a result of these prohibitions and distortions, aggravated in some cases by the passivity of the 'uninvolved bystanders' (Davies and Frawley, 1994) – adults who are aware of the trauma and who refuse to denounce it or protect the child. The environment thus becomes an accomplice to paralysis and silence.

As a direct result of silencing and stigmatization, shame often emerges. Shame is, along with fear, one of our oldest emotions and has been considered by some authors as a core element of trauma and its long-term consequences (Benau, 2023; Herman, 2015). Shame provokes the feeling of having something inside that no one can see, understand, or share. The subject feels the need to hide the trauma or to isolate defensively.

Trauma-related shame is often an isolated affective core, dissociated from the rest of one's self-experience. Early relational traumas are frequently linked to shame because they involve an interpersonal paradox: trusted caregivers are the very same ones who humiliate, endanger, or harm the individual. This paradox is often resolved only by self-attributing responsibility: the reason this happened must be me: "Attachment trauma comes from the one on whom one's sense of self-worth depends and, experienced through the ego centrism of the child, it is felt to be about the self, not the perpetrator" (Hill, 2015, p. 186).

Lack of recognition, disempowerment, and shame can add to dissociation, and push the victim to silence. This is paralleled in horror films by the absence of symbolic/societal recognition of the threat that protagonists' face, or by the failure of authority figures to explain and give meaning to what is happening – it is an absence of structures (in institutions, culture, society and others) to understand, support, regulate, or name the protagonists' pain.

The absence of a third figure (often the father) and the inoperability of authority figures and institutions in horror cinema are reminiscent of Benjamin's considerations of the failure of recognition that is at the core of trauma (Benjamin, 2017). Trauma experience is predicated on one or more harms to which is added an absence of containing, regulating, or acknowledging responses (see also Atwood & Stolorow, 2014). The absence of these responses, in the family or institutional sphere, aggravates the traumatic experience because it deprives the subjects of an opportunity to trust again in the expected and just order that should govern human bonds. Sometimes, this absence of responses is precisely because there are no structures of knowledge in the culture that recognize or name the harm the victims face (for example, the grief felt by homosexuals when they lost a partner to AIDS in the 1980s, or the experiences of 'sexual harassment' suffered by women on a daily basis before this category was coined in the 1970s). A form of violence based on categories of knowledge (or lack thereof) occurs: epistemic injustice (Fricker, 2007). The violation of the expectations (of care, reciprocity, or justice, among others) that sustain bonds goes unacknowledged in the environment, and the subject is deprived of an essential message: "you should have been treated differently," "you deserve to be protected." Horror film authorities who do not believe the story that the terrified protagonist tries to tell them, who are late to recognize or ignorant of the threat lurking around the corner, who stigmatize the protagonists or offer protection that fails and leads to an increase in the threat, explore this phenomenology. In these films, the supernatural threat is a significant dose of danger, but it is also experienced by the victims under the aggravating effects of loneliness, stigma, or collective indifference. The function of the 'Third,' which, according to Benjamin, makes it possible to review the damage suffered within a dialogue that recognizes the dignity of the individual and their right to better treatment, thus fails (2017). It is only from this position, the author argues, that there is hope for traumatized people to re-enter a shared space of trust.

A variation of this problem is presented in films where one or more children live engulfed in a symbiotic and toxic relationship with a single parent, without access to the separation, protection, and recognition as a separate person that a triangular structure (the existence of more than one main caregiver) or a network of care on a collective level often offers. Here there is another kind of failure of the third party that brings with it a form of trauma where the traumatic damage to the person does not reach the external realm or the public gaze. Films such as *Goodnight Mommy* (Franz & Fiala, 2014), *Black Swan* (Aronofsky, 2010), *The Babadook*, (Kent, 2014), *Psycho* (Hitchcock, 1960), *Run* (Chaganty, 2020) or *Carrie* (de Palma, 1976), are some examples. The trapped children in these films face a double danger: the danger that exists within their relationship with a demanding or aggressive mother, together with the danger of not being able to get their cry for help heard by the outside world – not being able to communicate what is happening to them. This difficulty in communicating harm and fear is also the subject of other horror film tropes, which we explore in the following section.

As mentioned above, under these conditions, it is very difficult for the mind to record the traumatic experience in a format that lends itself to (re)processing and, in the long term, integration.

Trauma as a disruption in the registering of experience

Freezing, not feeling, keeping quiet, are desperate strategies of self-protection that, in the short term, offer a sense of balance in the midst of an unbearable situation, as suggested by Glen Gabbard:

> Dissociation allows individuals to retain the illusion of psychological control when they experience a sense of helplessness and loss of control over their bodies. Dissociative defenses serve the dual function of helping victims to escape from the traumatic event while it is happening […].
>
> (2014, p. 374)

The cost of dissociating, however, has already been described: when the mind is deactivated, the mental processes by which meaning is constructed are also suspended. Subjects are unable to understand what is happening, activate an adaptive action plan (for example, flee, defend themselves, ask for help) and place the event in relation to the rest of their lives: "In an unspeakable state of terror, when the experience does not fit into the existing conceptual framework, that is, when it is lived in the register of the Real, the experience cannot be assimilated […]" (Boulanger, 2011, p. 131).

The impossibility of the mind to process what happens does not prevent it from being recorded. The psyche is forced to give the experience "some status – some 'inscription' – but without being able to give it the characteristics of a processable representation" (Benyakar & Lezica, 2005, p. 112).

Once again, Stephen King offers us a lucid view on this issue:

> [Terror] often arises from a pervasive sense of disestablishment; that things are in the unmaking. If that sense of unmaking is sudden and seems personal – if it hits you around the heart – then it lodges in the memory as a complete set.
>
> (1981, p. 30)

Memories are, at their most essential, adaptive tools. Our memory allows us to employ past learning in making decisions about what the present means and how we should respond to it. As has been said, human beings understand the present and respond to it by relying on metaphor. The point of a memory, therefore, is to remain accessible for use in the present and in the face of novel situations.

Traumatic memories, however, are not easily retrieved, and resist the mental processes by which we usually order our past experience. Research indicates that individuals with PTSD experience significant cognitive deficits related to memory processing, making it difficult for them to recall and narrate their traumatic experiences in an orderly fashion. Traumatized people have great difficulty in voluntarily remembering their traumas and making an orderly narrative of them: the memory is inaccessible, isolated from the network of contents of the self and, unlike these contents, resists the control of consciousness.

At the same time, the traumatic memory has the capacity to return unexpectedly and violently. It overpowers subjective experience, causing the person to have a sense of being *there again*. Traumatic memory is more vivid and violent than ordinary memories, which are more subject to the softening effect of the years and the 'conversation' we have with ourselves and others. Increased levels of adrenaline and other stress hormones in the system (something that happens when we are confronted with dangerous events or are in a state of alert) cause a particularly strong impression of memories (van der Kolk, 2015).

Studies have shown that trauma impacts the hippocampus, a brain region that is crucial for forming and retrieving episodic memories. PTSD is associated with structural abnormalities in the hippocampus, such as reduced volume, which impair these memory processes (Perl et al., 2023). Additionally, the posterior cingulate cortex (PCC), which plays a key role in narrative comprehension and autobiographical memory processing, also shows altered function and connectivity in individuals with PTSD. These alterations contribute to the fragmented and disorganized nature of traumatic memories, making them difficult to integrate into a coherent narrative (Perl et al., 2023).

Research by Perl and colleagues (2023) and J.C. Scott and colleagues (2015) supports the finding that PTSD-related memory deficits extend beyond the traumatic event itself, affecting everyday event processing and memory. This broader impact on cognitive function underscores the challenges that traumatized individuals face in voluntarily recalling and organizing their memories (Pitts et al., 2022).

Detached from the rest of the material of consciousness and resistant to narrative activity and biographical integration, traumatic contents have an anomalous status, a mixture of internal material and external impact, of their own and other people's reality. Despite coming from within, when they present themselves (in the form of dreams, flashbacks, or intrusive memories of the trauma) these contents may be subjectively experienced as having an external, persecutory nature. Trauma is registered as an 'exogenous intimacy.'

This brings us back to the aforementioned paradox of traumatic 'knowledge', where the alien, external character of memories is combined with the strength of their inscription in memory. This contradiction is a prime example of the internal breaks in the mind that are caused by trauma, and led van der Kolk to state that "traumatized people simultaneously remember too little and too much" (2015, p. 476).

The resistance of traumatic memory to access and control, and its ability to return in the form of a hyper-real version of the trauma, are features with a well-studied neurological basis. Research shows us that the brains of PTSD patients, when they remember their traumas, show a very particular pattern of activation: the limbic areas of the brain are over-activated, while there is reduced activity in the prefrontal area.

The limbic area is the seat of our most primary emotional system, the place where our survival-related emotions are 'produced.' Within the limbic system, the amygdala functions as a kind of "smoke detector" (van der Kolk, 2015) that quickly and automatically assesses what is painful or threatening, and triggers very rapid responses in preparation for attack or flight. Increased heart rate, hyperventilation, increased muscle tension, etc., are all part of this amygdala survival plan, along with the behavior that saves us (for example, jumping to protect us from a snake bite). Because the amygdala processes sensory information faster than the prefrontal brain, it decides whether situations pose a threat to our survival even before we are aware of the danger. By the time we realize what is happening, our body has probably already reacted.

Horror films have been able to instrumentalize this biological infrastructure, employing stimuli and visual configurations that 'touch' the amygdala directly and cause us to cringe in our seats, startle, or be surprised by the sound of our screaming before we even realize that we are screaming (Clasen, 2017). The montage and visual narrative tricks with which horror films exploit the workings of our limbic system are (among others): the deployment of incomplete stimuli that suggest danger (for example, dark, fuzzy shots with fragments of what could be an aggressor or a monster walking in the shadows); the sudden, close-up appearance of staring faces, teeth, bloodshot eyes, decomposing bodies, etc.; the transformation of seemingly innocuous stimuli (what looked like a friend's arm) into aberrant objects (the arm is revealed to be the friend's severed limb) (Clasen, 2017).

In constant interaction with the limbic system are the frontal lobes of the neocortex (the most modern and superficial layer of our brain). Unlike the amygdala (which processes stimuli quickly, globally, and unconsciously), the frontal cortex is responsible for processing information slowly, sequentially, and consciously in order to understand what is happening and derive learning that allows us to make medium or long-term adaptations from this understanding. This constant neural 'conversation' between an area responsible for making us feel and another that allows us to think produces a balanced experience of the self and a capacity to adapt to the environment.

As noted, the PTSD victim is trapped in an internal power imbalance: the limbic-cortical conversation has broken down. The limbic system, over-activated, hijacks brain functioning. The voice of fear, represented by the amygdala, 'screams' inside the brain. Faced with the memory of trauma, victims are deprived of the rational voice, which would normally make realistic discriminations between memory and perception (*it is not happening, it belongs to the past*), or between automatic defensive actions and adaptive planning (*you do not need to run or attack*). Reflection, planning, or abstract thinking become inaccessible for orientation in these moments of post-traumatic re-experiencing. Resistant to reflection and voluntary control, traumatic memories escape their encapsulation and burst into our subjectivity with overwhelming force, causing us to feel as we did in the original traumatic situation: terrified and helpless. They are a kind of 'pure present' in their ability to make us relive the original pain and fear.

Trauma penetrates the system and remains engraved in the psyche as an intimate and at the same time exogenous content. Throughout history, the internal-but-foreign nature of traumatic re-experiencing has been expressed through different metaphors and terms, such as "teratoma" (Ferenczi, 1933), and "foreign body" (Janet, 1907). Some trauma victims allude to sensations, memories, and emotions that dwell within the subjective experience but are disconnected from the rest of the contents of the self and have a kind of mechanics of their own. The traumatic content is there, inside, and at the same time it is not entirely recognizable as one's own.

An interesting representation of this phenomenon appears in *Sputnik* (Abramenko, 2020). The film tells the story of Konstantin, a Russian cosmonaut who, in the middle of the Cold War, returns from a mission harboring an alien creature that has invaded his body while he was in outer space. The creature is reminiscent, in some respects, of the xenomorph in *Alien* (R. Scott, 1979): it takes up residence in its host's body, from which it feeds and within which it grows. In this case, however, alien and human develop a symbiotic biology, so that at a certain point neither can survive without the other. No separation is possible, despite the Soviet military's attempts to extract the host to weaponize it against their American opponents.

This relates to the fact that the alien creature is symbolically linked to an emotional wound of Konstantin's: the discovery, a few days before his blast-off into space, that he has an unacknowledged son, locked up in a Russian orphanage. And this resonates with his own experience of orphanhood. The third orphan in this triangle – and also raised in an institution – is Tatyana, the co-protagonist of this story, a psychologist charged with unravelling the nature of the parasite from space. Tatyana discovers that the alien feeds, inside Konstantin, on his cortisol (a beautiful detail when we know that cortisol is one of the hormones responsible for fear).

Certain characteristics of the creature link it directly to the trauma of its host and to that of the co-protagonist. The creature leaves the host's body when the host sleeps and is phobic of sunlight: both traits are paradigmatic of mental contents that are defensively repressed. On the other hand, it behaves violently when outside, feeding on other human beings whom it brutally devours, which reminds us of another of the dissociated aspects of trauma that is, nevertheless, always ready to reemerge: rage. The alien is a crippled creature that crawls and struggles to stand on its two legs, something it has in common with the institutionalized, wheelchair-bound child we are shown in several of the film's flashbacks (and who, we later discover, is Tatyana as a child). The child is thus a mirror of Konstantin's abandoned son, as much as of Tatyana's abandonment trauma.

Symbols of the immutability of trauma

One of the ways in which horror represents this immutability of the painful past is the presence, in a significant number of films, of objects or spaces that are preserved intact in the lives of the characters. There are many examples of this phenomenon in the history of cinematic horror: the photo album preserved as a relic; the unaltered room of the dead; the closed and immutable attic or basement; a doll; a portrait or a piece of jewelry that holds meaning and represents something that happened and that still exerts its power over the characters. In the face of the story and the characters' progression through time, these relics preserve a fixed, unaltered moment. A significant amount of emotional resonance – often traumatic – is condensed in them. These relics function as signifiers of experiences that have been, like the traumatic memory, isolated from the ordinary temporal flow and preserved in their original potency. From the anomalous place they occupy, memories of trauma cast their shadow over individuals in the present, without lending themselves to the transformative play of metaphor, and resisting re-transcription. The traumatic past functions as a *present* for the victims. In terms of predictive processing, traumatic contents have such a high intensity and affective salience that they function as rigid priors, hardly susceptible to updating in the face of novel stimuli and prediction errors (Kube et al., 2020). At the same time, the relics of horror cinema are always close to the characters, lurking over the story. The protagonists come into contact with these objects as if they were peering into an uncanny diorama, inside which the past remains intact and absorbing.

For example, in *The Changeling*, the room where the child was murdered is preserved in its original appearance, isolated in a hidden attic at the top of the house (Medak, 1980). In the same film, the ball that belonged to the protagonist's dead daughter is an intact remnant of the lost past. One of the opening scenes presents us with the protagonist's memory of his daughter throwing the ball to him. Later, tormented by grief, the man decides to dispose of the object by throwing it into a river. In the next scene, however, the ball, wet from the river's waters, descends the stairs towards the man as soon as he enters the house.

During the first act of *Psycho*, we are introduced to Norman Bates' disturbing hobby: he embalms and preserves, in a state almost identical to the original, dead animals (Hitchcock, 1960). As the story unfolds, we discover that this habit hides a more sinister preservation: that of the body of his deceased mother. Norman himself reproduces the effigy of his mother in his own body, by dressing in her clothes and committing the murderous acts that she, had she been alive, would have committed. In the ramshackle Bates Motel, young Norman's traumatic past is preserved in its original intensity and quality.

The protagonist who gives her name to *What Ever Happened to Baby Jane?* was a blonde showgirl, adored by the audience and her parents, but who is now a forgotten, decrepit actress (Aldrich, 1962). The elderly Jane walks in front of her house's mirrors holding a doll that represents her as a small, radiant girl: the child protagonist of a lost paradise. As the story progresses, Jane's efforts to do her hair and makeup just like her doll's gradually lead to a fusion between character and object (i.e., between present and past) with uncanny overtones.

In *The Devil's Backbone,* there is a howitzer embedded in the courtyard of the orphanage (del Toro, 2001). The shell fell on the same night as the murder of one of the children at the orphanage, and is a camouflaged reminder of the unacknowledged crime, a kind of totem with which the children are fascinated, without knowing what meanings are contained within it.

In *The Village*, each of the leaders of the isolated rural community where the story takes place has a black box in their living room. Inside these locked boxes, their memories of the atrocious deaths of their loved ones are preserved (Shyamalan, 2004). And in *Lake Mungo*, a mobile phone buried in the desert holds images of the protagonist's encounter with a specter of singularly traumatic significance (Anderson 2008).

The basement is another of the most important metaphors for the anomalous inscription of traumatic experiences and their immutability. Basements (and their variations) are regions relatively immune to the passage of time, maintaining the status of a frozen scene or stage, containing unprocessed material from the past. Despite being hidden, they are – literally – at the base of the building, underpinning the entire home (just as the traumatic underlies much of the mental life and behavior of some victims). As a hidden emotional core, these rooms articulate a large part of the characters' movements and lives: *you must not pass through here*; *it is forbidden to play here*; *from a certain time of day, this place is dangerous.*

The trope appears in an overwhelming number of films, from which we have selected a few examples. One of the first discoveries the girls make when they move into their new house in *The Conjuring* is a boarded-up basement, where the memories of an atrocious past are still alive (Wan, 2013). This is also the case in *The Changeling,* where the dissociated traumatic is hidden, this time, in the attic of the house (where the boy was drowned) and in an underground well (where his body was left) (Medak, 1980). When the source of her terrible dreams is revealed to Nancy in *A Nightmare on Elm Street*, she finds the evidence of the silenced past in a furnace in the basement of her house (Craven, 1984). It is there that she herself will later be haunted by Krueger.[2] Norman's dead and preserved mother sits in the basement of *Psycho* (Hitchcock, 1960), waiting to be discovered (or, failing that, to be able to continue committing her aggressions). The death of an innocent child in *The Devil's Backbone* is submerged in the water of a cistern beneath the orphanage (del Toro, 2001). The dark *doppelgängers* of the families in *Us* come from a parallel, grey society that dwells in the subsoil of the world (Peele, 2019). The atrocities committed by the demonic clown in *It*, like the memory of other crimes committed in the town of Derry, are hidden in the deepest recesses of its sewers (Muschietti,

2017). In an interesting variation on the trope, *Dark Water* locates the place of the dissociated in the water tank on the roof of a building where a girl, neglected by her parents, fell and drowned (Nakata, 2002).

Another classic variation is presented by *The Shining*, where the space of traumatic inscription is a building in its entirety (Kubrick, 1980). The Overlook Hotel, by virtue of some kind of power that is never defined in the film – nor in the Stephen King novel that inspired it (1977) – has the capacity to register the human misfortunes that occurred in its rooms, halls, and corridors. The specters of men and women who were victims of various atrocities wander around the hotel under the gaze of the characters who have a gift for seeing them (Danny, and his father Jack), while they try to draw father and son into the 'other' existence in which they find themselves.

The horror house has sometimes also functioned as a representative of a frozen time that resists change. Stephen King describes haunted house stories as tales of the 'Bad Place', that is, of a space that contains and retains some negative force (1981). Often this force is the result of unexpiated crimes, unacknowledged harms, or the transgenerational reproduction of one form of violence or another. The Bad Place is often the seat of trauma.

Charles Derry argues that the horror of many of these stories rests on the tension between a stagnated emotional time and the present time of the world, which keeps moving forward (2009). In the encounter of both forms of temporality, the dramatic (and terrifying) tension of these stories appears: "Usually the house is a dead thing, containing memories, corpses, or reminders of an old way of life; the horror usually arises because, while the times change, the house and its occupants do not" (Derry, 2009, p. 47).

These and other examples refer to an idea that is a common denominator of the genre: the fragmentation of space as a metaphor for the fragmentation of the mind into visible (conscious) and hidden (unconscious) areas. This splitting of mental contents (paralleled by a splitting of physical spaces in the horror narrative) is usually the result of a painful, unacceptable past that was expelled from consciousness and that, from its shadowy corner, keeps coming back.

Notes

1 A dramatic example is provided by some victims of sexual abuse who reveal, with great shame, that during the trauma their bodies responded with involuntary patterns of sexual arousal.
2 It is of particular interest that, just when we think the psychological architecture of the story has reached its maximum depth, Nancy discovers that her basement hides a door to a second, deeper basement, which she must enter to save herself. The film seems to suggest something that is a relatively standard argument in psychoanalysis: the unconscious is organized vertically, in progressively deeper layers of conflicts and repressions.

Chapter 2

Traumatic fragmentation in modern horror cinema

Under healthy conditions, our mental functioning manifests as a dialogue between various functions that, despite being distinct, coordinate to create a unified experience of the self and a coherent perception of the world. For instance, memory (relating to the past) interacts with perception (of the present) to help us interpret our surroundings and current events. Affect meets reason (assisting in organizing our emotional life); conversely, thought is influenced by emotion (which provides energy and tone to our actions). The different versions of who we are (our multiple selves) 'talk' to each other, so that we experience our identity as a fluid yet stable solution of voices that make us who we are. The mind is an interweaving of melodies that, being distinct and always maintaining a state of relative tension, manage to sound in a harmonious way.

As we shall see in the following pages, trauma attacks this daily interrelation of mental contents and functions.

Psychic fragmentation is another core feature of the phenomenology of trauma. It is an effect of excessive pressure on the traumatized mind, in the same way that the walls of a building that supports too much weight fracture. But it is also an act of self-protection: in a desperate attempt to survive emotionally, our psyche splits (Bromberg, 2011; Fairbairn, 1952a; Schwartz, 2000).

Traumatic mental fragmentation has various manifestations, some of which have become essential tropes of modern horror cinema. In the following pages, we review seven aspects of post-traumatic fragmentation that frequently circulate in modern horror films.

A disconnect between memory and perception

As previously developed, our mind functions as an 'analogy machine' that constantly employs comparisons between now and before to interpret the meaning of experience and deploy adaptive responses (Hofstadter & Sander, 2013; Modell, 1997; Modell, 2005; Modell, 2009). This can be understood as the result of a basic process that affects all living organisms: the imperative to create (and test, repeatedly) predictive models of the world that, on the basis of prior learning, allow for anticipating outcomes, detecting prediction errors, and reducing uncertainty

(A. Clark, 2013; Hohwy, 2013). The metaphorical game is bidirectional: the past colors the meaning of what is happening in the present, but the present also alters the meaning of past experiences. Thanks to our metaphorical capacity, we can establish both similarities between separate moments in our biography and nuances and differences, and so what happens to us can serve to transform, retroactively, the meaning of what happened to us. For example, for the individual who was harshly treated at the hands of their parents, experiencing healthy and balanced conflicts within an adult relationship based on trust can help them to positively redefine their identity and experience of conflict within close relationships. Thanks to this 're-transcription' of the past under the influence of the present, some of our most difficult old experiences change their meaning and become more tolerable.

Moreover, memories are constantly reprocessed and transformed, as they are connected to the subject's vast network of knowledge about themself and the world. If we were to ask several people about an event they experienced together some years ago, each of them would share with us a different memory. Their minds, rather than preserving the experience in its original form, have reconstructed it by adding nuances, combining it with other memories, and filtering it through their values and other sources of personal meaning. This reconstruction process is influenced by schemas – cognitive structures that help individuals organize and interpret information. Schemas can fill in gaps and make memories more coherent, often leading to the incorporation of biases and errors. For instance, a study by F.C. Bartlett (1932) showed that participants altered stories when retelling them over time, incorporating their own biases and existing knowledge structures to make the narrative more consistent with their understanding (van der Linden & Schapiro, 2017). The mere fact of recounting what happened alters the memory, as the narrative constantly reorders the experience, selects what is important, and molds it in different ways on each occasion. Memory is a plastic content, a socially constructed material that undergoes modifications in each of the communicative acts used to share it. The retroactive influence of today on yesterday constantly reactivates our identity, allowing it to be a living thing. We cannot go back to where we have been.

Trauma precisely undermines the metaphorical, dynamic character of our memory. As has been said, under the influences of freezing and silencing, the experience of trauma can be stored in a kind of isolated corner, a basement of the mind. Encapsulated and separated from the web of content that shapes our identity, the traumatic memory resists change. The creative tension between who we were and who we are is interrupted, and a painful split opens up between the past and the present. The opportunity to draw similarities and make comparisons is lost. Like an insect trapped in amber, trauma maintains its original state.

The images, smells, sounds, and bodily sensations, as well as the emotions associated with the event, retain the same quality and equivalent intensity over the years. This makes the memory more – actual, reenacted – experience than memory, more present than past. According to Dori Laub, these reminiscences retain "their magnetic power in their contradictory detail and persistent clarity and in the concomitant dense, yet absorbing opaqueness that enshrouds" (2005, p. 312). If we stated that ordinary memory is flexible and socially constructed, traumatic memory is rigid, isolated, and incommunicable: "for many other adult survivors of massive trauma, memories are not mediated by subsequent events; they remain intact, in an endless feedback loop, as if time had stopped" (Boulanger, 2011, p. 20).

We explained at the beginning that, under healthy mental functioning, metaphor works as a detector of analogies and also of differences. This would make it possible, for example, to recognize the distance that exists between a present moment (for example, an argument with a partner, in which the latter raises their voice) and a painful moment in the past (for example, an abusive parent who raised their voice just before resorting to violence against the child). When the memory is traumatic, the metaphor tends to become rigid and only similarities are perceived: the screaming partner of today *is* the screaming parent of the past. Under the anomalous temporality of trauma, the metaphor tends to fixate and freeze as it loses its playful aspect, and, therefore, the individual feels a more rigid fit between the present and the past (Modell, 2005). These difficulties affecting the temporal construction of memories have been articulated with particular clarity by Dent:

> In trauma, the neural markers that normally give us the feeling that an image, sensation, thought, or emotion belongs to the past fail to be encoded. As a result, traumatic memories do not carry the feeling of something recalled; instead, they feel here and now […]. This quality creates confusion and terror even when images intrude that cannot belong to current reality, as in a nighttime flashback. It becomes even more difficult when emotions or sensations arise in full force in the present – you are terrified, panicked, alone, threatened, in physical pain. Everything in your awareness screams danger, now, and it's almost impossible to sustain a sense of safety. Even if you can summon the idea that the danger belongs to the past – a thought that demands a fair amount of knowledge and presence – nothing in your body believes it
>
> (2020, p. 441)

The current situation is experienced as a pure repetition of the past. There is a sense of total equivalence: it is the *same*, and it is happening *now*. The exchange between the two timelines is interrupted, and the past is immutable. The traumatic memory is thus a frozen piece of personal history.

When the experience is constructed in this manner (as re-experiencing rather than remembering), the traumatic memory is re-inscribed, creating a vicious cycle reminiscent of the rigidity with which curses and supernatural threats are portrayed in horror films. Cyclicality and repetition – as will be developed in detail in later sections – are defining markers of horror stories. Something dreadful tends to return on every anniversary or across successive generations of the same family or village. If those affected by this threat do nothing effective to deal with it, the threat always returns with the same intensity (as long as there is no reprocessing): it is a pure present relived.

Stephen King's story *Sometimes They Come Back* represents this poignantly. Its protagonist, Jim Norman, is a high school teacher who is still plagued by nightmares replaying a tragic scene from his childhood: he and his older brother were assaulted by three juvenile delinquents, and his brother was stabbed to death while Jim managed to escape. None of the killers were caught. Many years later, the feelings experienced at the time are reactivated every time Jim witnesses a scene of bullying at school, causing him to collapse. When he finally seems recovered and able to cope with his life normally, three new students show up to his English class for troubled students; they are, to Jim's shock and horror, the same three boys who took his brother's life and who, he is convinced, are now coming back for him. The biggest shock, of course, comes from the fact that all three are exactly the same age as when the attack occurred, despite the time that has passed, because – as the character will find out after some quick research – they are all dead: they died in a car accident shortly after his brother's death. These bullies who return from Jim's nightmares perfectly exemplify the way in which traumatic experiences can be preserved in memory and 'resurrected' with the clarity and emotional intensity of a present-day experience.

Clotted affect and other resistances

Time, as we have said, transforms memory by connecting it to new experiences. Past experience, in contact with reality, is forced to change in intensity and meaning. However, the mind of those who have traumatically lost someone may want to defend itself against these natural evolutions of memory. Some horror films offer an interesting exploration of this phenomenon. In them, characters, devastated by loss, resist saying goodbye to the deceased and mourning. At the heart of these stories is a conflict between living in the present and clinging to a past that one does not wish to relinquish.

Don't Look Now (Roeg, 1973) is well-known film that explores this issue. Based on Daphne Du Maurier's story *Don't Look Now* (whose title probably evokes the condition Hades gave Orpheus when he allowed him to attempt to bring his dead beloved out of the underworld and back to life), it is a story about traumatic grief. Haunted by the tragic drowning of their daughter, John Baxter and his wife Laura move to Venice in the hope that a change of location will help them to free themselves from grief. In a restaurant, two elderly women approach them with the news that their daughter may still be alive; one of them, blind, claims to have seen her. From there begins to unfold a story where, once again, the boundaries between the fantasized and the real become blurred (is that small figure scurrying through the canals in the red raincoat not the missing daughter?), and the past becomes dangerously intertwined with the present (why does John see his wife dressed in mourning, crying on a boat? Is it a premonition of a second death to come?). The film's narrative is deliberately messy, strewn with loose impressions and terrifying snippets – as traumatic memory is – and deeply uncomfortable until the fatal climax, in which John believes he has, at last, found his daughter.

Horror has presented us with other stories of parental grief (perhaps the most traumatic form of loss imaginable), in films where grieving parents receive a supernatural invitation to retrieve the child. This always leads to an uncanny outcome. So it does in both versions of *Pet Sematary* (Lambert, 1989; Kolsch and Widmyer, 2019), in which Louis Creed buries the body of his recently deceased child in an animal cemetery in the woods, which is known to allow the dead pets that are buried there to come back to life. Something similar happens to the protagonists of *Godsend* (Hamm, 2004), when a doctor – played by Robert De Niro – offers to clone their son Adam, recently killed in a car accident.

The child, after their burial in the magical graveyard or their passage through cloning, returns to the life of their devastated parents. This return, however, comes at a price; we soon discover that the resurrected child is not an exact version of the one who left. In this reading of Promethean myth, freezing time is an achievement reserved for the gods, and when humans aspire to it, they open the door to a terrible threat.

We almost always encounter this catalogue of resistances in the context of deaths which, because of their premature or violent nature, have been traumatic for the survivor. Traumatic grief is almost always a blocked grief. Freud's concept of melancholic obstinacy describes how traumatic grief can prevent the natural progression of mourning. This coagulates the person's emotions and prevents the natural progression of grief towards a resolution (S. Freud, 1917/1945). These people find it difficult to say goodbye to the deceased, to relocate them to a new place and thus resume the course of their own lives. As if it were a current presence, the dead casts a shadow over the Ego, contaminating the experience of the present. This theory has been expanded and supported by subsequent research, highlighting that traumatic grief often results in blocked grief, where individuals struggle to symbolically say goodbye to the deceased. The dead person's memory remains ever-present, overshadowing the mourner's self and contaminating their present experiences (Hall, 2014). Neuroimaging studies further demonstrate that the brain's processing of grief involves areas linked to emotion regulation and memory, supporting Freud's view that unresolved grief can profoundly affect one's emotional and cognitive functioning (Ong, Fuller-Rowell, & Bonanno, 2018).

This dynamic is often fueled, as has been noted, by the complicated nature of these losses. Melancholy often occurs when the deceased and the survivor shared an ambivalent bond: a complicated mixture of love and hate; desire intertwined with rejection; a suffocating co-dependency, among other confusing emotions. These ambivalences of the actual relationship can be internalized as a split between an exciting object and a rejecting object (Fairbairn, 1952a). Emotionally attached to both objects, the person suffers an internal split between anger towards the object that frustrates and longing for the object that promises or seduces. This internal oscillation complicates the mourning process and prevents the individual from moving forward.

At other times, melancholy may result from the fact that the death of the deceased provokes intense feelings of guilt. When grief is intertwined with guilt, it can be particularly difficult to distance oneself from the dead person, who ends up taking up too much psychic space. It is as if, driven by guilt, the survivor feels compelled to give a large part of their mental life to the dead person. In turn, such a sense of being occupied by the internal image of the deceased can generate intense anger towards this 'parasitic' emotional presence. This would increase the original feelings of guilt and thus reinforce the melancholic circuit.

This phenomenology is at the heart of the romantic conflict in *Bram Stoker's Dracula*, Francis Ford Coppola's 1992 approximation of the vampire myth. In Coppola's version, Count Dracula is a subject trapped in an inescapable melancholic loop, and his immortality is a very direct metaphor for his inability to detach himself from the pain of his beloved's violent death. In the course of his medieval struggle against the Turks, the latter send false missives to his castle telling of his death on the battlefield, leading his wife Elisabeta to commit suicide. Returning from the war, Dracula finds his wife's corpse under the altar. In the eyes of Dracula, God has turned his back on him and rewarded his sacrifice by taking away his most precious possession. The Count is thus faced with a complicated mixture of grief over Elisabeta's death, guilt for not having been there to prevent her suicide, and anger towards the forces that have orchestrated his misfortune. Traumatic grief thus begins, metaphorized as the surrender of Dracula's soul to the forces of hell, and his condemnation to roam the earth for all eternity bound to an unresolved loss and a thirst to regain lost love. Coppola's undead is a melancholic, empty, wandering being. He is perpetually attached to the idealized image of an object that, despite having disappeared from reality, has become firmly embedded at the core of the self, enslaving it.

We are shown a similar conflict (albeit armed with a very different aesthetic) in *The Skin I Live In* (Almodóvar, 2011) – a film that, despite its psychological thriller aspect, was defined by its director as "a scary film without scares or screams." The protagonist of this film – inspired by *Les Yeux Sans Visage* (Franju, 1960) – is Robert Ledgard, a plastic surgeon with a history of accumulated traumas: the betrayal of his wife, her subsequent death by suicide, the rape of his daughter, and, finally, her suicide. Wracked by these wounds, he tries to win his wife back in a gruesome way. Using genetic manipulation techniques that allow him to mold human skin, he transforms the body of his daughter's rapist (whom he has previously kidnapped) into a copy of his wife. The metamorphosis reaches terrifying heights when the surgeon subjects his hostage to a sex change, which includes a vaginoplasty and the production of artificial breasts, the grafting of female hair, and the general alteration of his features. The young man ends up becoming a woman-object, a body-thing that reproduces the dead wife.

This story aptly reflects the intertwining of grief and trauma mentioned above. For Ledgard, the loss of his wife and daughter is more than a cause for grief. These deaths bring a complicated mix of emotions, including guilt (for not having been an adequate husband; for not having been able to protect his child from rape) and anger (towards his wife, whose death is linked to her infidelity). Ledgard's violence against the bodies – particularly the body of the young man whom he transforms into a copy of his wife – is a massive denial of loss and of his own responsibility for the deaths of both women. In this melancholic solution, the production of an object identical to the lost one functions as a total defense, an act that slows down the passage of time and obstructs the process of mourning.

Post-traumatic fragmentations of identity (I): Survival by self-division

In the face of trauma, the mind may 'choose' to break down its subjective experience into isolated chunks of feeling and thinking. At a subclinical or 'normal' level, individuals employ dissociative, self-fragmentation strategies in a balanced and relatively flexible manner. These strategies are basic tools for the day-to-day management of experiences that are too overwhelming, unpleasant, or difficult to incorporate into one's self-image. Towards the zone of greater severity, these mechanisms function as "the only safeguard against affective chaos" (Bromberg, 2009, p. 96). Under these conditions, dissociation may become chronic or operate with high rigidity and intensity, aiming to radically separate aspects of experience to protect the mind from the unbearable feelings provoked by trauma. Subjectivity is thus configured as an amalgam of discontinuous, divergent states that do not interact with each other. Through these internal exclusions, the individual manages to compartmentalize or dilute unmanageable feelings. The fragments of identity, isolated from each other, tend to multiply and acquire autonomy, developing 'a mind of their own.' As described by van der Kolk, "Dissociation is the essence of trauma. The overwhelming experience is split off and fragmented, so that the emotions, sounds, images, thoughts, and physical sensations related to the trauma take on a life of their own" (2015, p. 174)

In contrast to the essentially integrated quality that characterizes the healthy mind (a network of self-states that are diverse and at the same time connected), insecurity tends to produce a solution of isolated forms of experience of self and others. Isolation, as mentioned above, is a defensive motivation: to take unbearable aspects of one's experience or history out of the field, or to eradicate patterns of functioning that may expose the person to further repetitions of the trauma. The parent whose difficult past sometimes causes them to feel fierce envy towards his otherwise beloved child may strive to isolate these two emotions (envy and love) from each other, since, for them, recognizing both as essential parts of his parenting is very dangerous. The teacher who humiliates their students from a position of superiority may struggle to keep this version of themselves separate from another part that also defines their experience: the deep insecurity and fear of not measuring up.

Under the effect of a history of traumatic impacts, combined with a rigid use of the defensive fragmentation just described, the individual finds it difficult to maintain (and employ) a stable model of the social world. The mind assembles itself as a non-integrated solution of images, emotions, and tendencies that do not dialogue with each other, as well as representations of self and others that are incompatible and change dramatically: a fragmented mirror of the world. This fragmentation is particularly evident when levels of emotional intensity exceed a certain threshold of tolerance, in the context of intense attachment interactions, or when feelings or memories linked to an original trauma reappear.

These dissociative phenomena are characterized by compartmentalization (i.e., aspects of personal experience are isolated from the rest of the contents of identity), automaticity (i.e., some of these dissociative contents are suddenly triggered and escape the person's conscious control) and altered states of consciousness (i.e., when the dissociative trauma-related states come into play, the experience of oneself and the world tends to be limited, partial, or highly distorted) (Hill, 2015).

In *The Babadook* (Kent, 2014), for example, the mother's desire to protect the child and the mother's hatred are dissociated, so that, despite being aspects of the same experience (that of a mother suffering from complicated grief) the two aspects of the mother's experience do not get integrated. When maternal rejection is activated (in the film this is a response to the fact that the birth of the child coincided with – and indirectly caused – the death of the husband), this state bursts into the mother's subjective experience in an automatic, preverbal way, accompanied by strong distortions in her experience as a caregiver, and an uncontrollable impulse to harm the child. For this mother, the intensity of her grief makes it very difficult to integrate her love for her child with the negative feelings she has for him. Her experience of motherhood is (as in the case of so many other characters in the horror narrative) a 'broken mirror,' a solution of contradictory parts that do not allow themselves to be connected. The metaphor of the Babadook monster brings together these characteristics that are defining of dissociative posttraumatic states, and reflects (probably more accurately than any technical definition) the subjective experience of being visited by a reality that is within you but does not feel like your own, or being ravaged by terrifying affects that are difficult to understand.

One of the effects of dissociation is that the person oscillates between parts of their subjective experience that have been defensively separated. Subjective life is defined as a landscape of plots that, although belonging to the same field, have been hermetically fenced off and excluded from each other. Some interactions or some affective states can push people to move from one plot to another, which subjectively feels like a radical change in the way someone sees themselves and others. A video demonstration of transference-centred psychotherapy shows a thirty-four-year-old woman who comes to her session, in a clear nervous state because her partner has recently proposed to her, and asking her therapist (Frank Yeomans) for specific guidance on what she should do (APPIVideo, 2018). The patient's experience is that of being small in relation to an other (the therapist) who is perceived as omnipotent and capable of saving her. The therapist's neutral attitude, and his invitation to reflect together on this situation, makes the patient frustrated, and then something changes radically: the woman becomes hostile, calls the therapist an "idiot" and mocks his position and his work. Abruptly – and without awareness – there has been a leap between two incompatible models, a change without continuity. The patient has gone from being someone small (in relation to someone big and powerful) to experiencing herself as a fierce and aggressive person in relation to another who is despised and can be attacked. This example illustrates the combined appearance of several nuances of a traumatized identity: the defensive encapsulation of some parts, the abrupt reappearance of these parts under the effect of specific stimuli, and the experience (in the person as well as in others) of confusion and fragmentation. A "normal" disappointment can trigger dissociated traumatic feelings of rage and despair, and make what to many would be an ordinary and harmless episode be experienced by some people as equivalent to the original trauma (in the case in the example, the patient experiences her therapist as the omnipotent caregiver who abandons her and leaves her helpless and, alternatively, as a dangerous and despicable figure – a projected aspect of the self, likely – whom she is justified in harming).

These oscillations are reminiscent of the "drama triangle," a term coined by Stephen Karpman (1968) to refer to a system of sudden shifts between three different positions: 'victim,' 'aggressor,' and 'rescuer.' Traumatized individuals may shift between positions corresponding to each of these 'characters' of the triangle, so that at times they feel helpless against a persecutor they need protection from (victim), at other times they feels enraged and full of destructive hatred towards the other (aggressor), and, at other times, they see themselves as strong, immune, capable of rescuing others, who are experienced as small and fragile (saviour). In all cases, the changes from one self-state to another, rather than being part of a behavior under the individual's control, are states that *happen* to them.

According to Charles Derry (2009), symbols of identity are frequent in films concerned with the division of the psyche. Broken dolls, the cracks that divide walls and faces, the disconnection between spaces in the house (usually a bright, public area that conceals a dark, secret zone), etc., are part of the collection of images with which horror explores the traumatic division of the psyche. These symbols of identity are objects that represent some aspect of a character's tormented self or contain the dark or deviant aspects of the protagonist's personality. Consider one of the paradigmatic examples of this: the eponymous picture of Dorian Gray, which captures the protagonist's ageing, but also his darker drives, his selfishness, malice and envy (Wilde, 1890/2008). Photographs, puppets, dolls, statuettes, pieces of costume jewelry, and even pets can function as symbols of unrecognized aspects of the character's identity. Among them, Derry highlights the *mirror* as a symbol par excellence of mental fragmentation in horror films.

In horror films, mirrors often offer fragmentary reflections (for example, half of a face, a figure with its back turned) or multiple reflections. This kind of visual schizophrenia is almost a hallmark of the genre, often alluding to the fractured personalities of its protagonists or the decoupling between different timelines.

In *Black Swan* (Aronofsky, 2010), for example, we follow the story of a young ballerina whose early mechanisms of self-organization in the face of relational trauma prove flimsy, ultimately exposing a fragmentary structure. Nina lives alone under the control of Erica, her mother, who exercises total narcissistic and aggressive dominance over her: like a doll, she dresses and undresses her daily, directs her career, tightly controls her desires and sexuality, and keeps her confined in a pink room full of stuffed animals. In one scene, we discover that the bedroom of this possessive mother-witch is filled with self-portraits, confirming the essentially narcissistic nature of their relationship: Erica can only see herself.

As a victim of intolerable subjugation and emotional ambivalence within her relationship with her mother, and under the simultaneous effect of her father's abandonment, Nina's mind has been forced to dissociate into irreconcilable parts: childhood innocence (imposed by her controlling mother) and rage (resulting from her traumas and frustrations); love and hate; purity and sex. One of the film's posters, in fact, shows Nina's perfect face pierced by a vertical crack. Self-fragmentation becomes inoperative when Nina is tasked with playing the two leading roles in the ballet *Swan Lake*: the White Swan and the Black Swan. The challenge of simultaneously sustaining these two antagonistic characters (metaphors for the separate parts of her psyche) becomes problematic because, for Nina, defensive fragmentation has, for years, maintained her psychic organization. The effort to overcome this dissociation leads to a tragic outcome, despite Nina's efforts to bring the Black Swan to the surface without it destroying her.

The mirror, omnipresent throughout the film, reflects this internal disintegration of the mind. We see Nina multiplied in front of the mirror in her rehearsal room (often supervised by her mother). We see her in front of the mirrors in the dance hall at the theater, and in front of the bathroom mirror on which a fellow company member has written "whore" after Nina is cast in the lead role. During her commute on the subway, Nina faces the glass of the train, finding a darkened image of herself in the window. At the entrance to her flat, a circular mirror surrounded by small mirrors reflects her image in multiple directions (notably, this happens on the night she plunges into an adventure of drugs and sex with her colleague Lily). As the story moves towards its denouement, Nina finds herself between two mirrors that infinitely reproduce her image, and in a moment worthy of the best Freudian "*unheimlich*" (S. Freud, 1919/1945), she discovers that her reflection has taken on a life of its own, moving independently of her will. The mirrors in the film evolve in parallel to Nina's mental disorder: as the story progresses, they return an increasingly problematized image of the protagonist.

Figure 2.1 In *Black Swan* (Aronofsky, 2010), Nina faces a dark transformation (see the blackness spreading over her arm) related to the division of her psyche.

In *Mirrors* (Aja, 2008), trauma returns in the form of images from the past that impose themselves on the mirrors of the present: when the protagonist looks into these mirrors, he does not see himself, but the victims of unresolved atrocities, whom he must confront. In one of the most chilling scenes of *Twin Peaks* (Lynch, 1990), we discover that Laura Palmer's father contains within his personality 'Bob,' the supernatural killer responsible for Laura's death: both the father and the killer are aspects of the same split self.

In *Carrie* (de Palma, 1976), the protagonist, torn between obedience to her mother's excessive authority and the desire to go out into the world, fractures a mirror using her telekinetic abilities. In *The Shining* (Kubrick, 1980), the word "redrum," obsessively repeated by little Danny, acquires its meaning – and reveals the impulses hidden in the father's fragmented identity – when it is projected onto a mirror.

In *Midsommar* (Aster, 2019), the protagonist, tormented and guilt-ridden by her sister's suicide, encounters her sister's image in a mirror. In *Candyman* (Rose, 1992), the repeated utterance of the monster's name in front of a mirror serves to summon him. In the most recent revision of this story the mirror functions as a representative of the division between the visible face (ordered, integrated, and modern) and the buried face (tortured and exploited) of the African-American community in the United States (*Candyman*, DaCosta, 2021).

Poltergeist (Hooper, 1982) shows us a mirror capable of torturing one of the parapsychologists by presenting him with an image of his flayed face. In *Occulus* (Flannagan, 2013), two traumatized adults must confront their fears, which return – unsurprisingly – on the surface of a mirror. In *Repulsion* (Polanski, 1965), as her sister's wardrobe closes, Carol sees herself reflected in one of the door mirrors and, behind her, the image of the assailant who raped her years before. In *In a Glass Cage* (Villaronga, 1986), a mirror serves to offer two images of the Nazi doctor, now disabled and trapped within an iron lung: the image of the torturer of the past, and that of the victim of the present.

In *Red Dragon* (Ratner, 2002), the killer, a man who was subjected to severe emotional and physical abuse by his grandmother, deals with his feelings of traumatic helplessness and shame by embedding pieces of mirror in the eye sockets of his victims. The corpses, with this prosthesis, are passive beings who cannot avoid "seeing" him as someone powerful and strong: someone capable of dominating them.

We find the most pronounced manifestation of self-fragmentation in dissociative identity disorder (DID; formerly known as multiple personality disorder). People diagnosed with this condition experience themselves as inhabited or dominated by different personalities, also called 'alters,' each of them linked to different aspects of the traumatic drama: the impotent and frightened child; the enraged and vengeful victim; the persecutor or judge; the rescuer or protector; the uninvolved bystander; etc. These subjects have the impression that some of the dissociated selves that make up their personality struggle to gain control over their mind, in a fashion that reminds us of what happens in horror stories with regards to ghosts (and their efforts to haunt houses) or spirits (and their tendency to possess bodies). It is no coincidence, in fact, that one form of DID has been described as "possession"

(American Psychiatric Association [APA], 2013), where different identities appear as external agents that take control over the person. These 'invading' entities may be described as a supernatural being or spirit, or as another person (for example, a deceased relative). The statistical evidence correlating DID with trauma (particularly childhood sexual abuse) or unresolved early losses is overwhelming (Sinason, 2002). In many cases, childhood trauma is combined with the absence of protection and support from the environment, or the absence of support in processing the experience and constructing meaning for the trauma. Under these circumstances, the child must use his or her alters as transitional objects to help process this violent contact with reality.

Mental contents thus exist as a series of parallel voices. These voices, far from dialoguing with each other and weaving an integrated picture of the experience, form a cacophonous solution, sometimes so intolerable that the individual must keep them separate from each other. The memories of the traumatized self are separated from the 'official' image of the self, as the former (which include overwhelming feelings of smallness, dirt, shame, or loneliness, among others) are incompatible with the latter. The organization of self in a fragmentary architecture is, as has been repeatedly stated, a defensive solution, "a desperate effort to preserve life and sanity by constructing an identity to manage (for example, disown, compartmentalize, diffuse) pain, anxiety, terror, and shame" (Schwartz, 2000, pp. 4–5).

An obvious fictional interpretation of this phenomenon can be found in *Split* (Shyamalan, 2016). Kevin, a young man who was abused and neglected as a child, has his personality divided into a multiplicity of alters, who represent different aspects of his traumatic experience and compete with each other for control.

At a slightly greater metaphorical distance, *In My Skin* (de Van, 2002) offers an interesting representation of mental fragmentation in relation to trauma. The film begins with a credits sequence in which we are shown a screen divided into two halves and, above this split frame, a catalogue of images and their negatives. Here is the first statement of intent of this story, which is presented to us as an exploration of the psychic division into visible/civilized/light zones and hidden/primary/dark zones.

We soon discover that the trigger for this internal fragmentation is an apparently banal accident that Esther, the main character, suffers at a night party. Esther goes out into the courtyard of the house where the party is taking place, brushes against a sharp object, and injures her leg. The film seems to suggest that the accident in the courtyard is not the trauma, but the trigger of a previous traumatic process, which was hidden and is somehow unveiled by the accident. Several scenes show us Esther in relationships (friendship, work, and romantic) defined by the subjugation and imposition that others exert over her. It is a series of episodes of hidden, implicit demands that, in their repetition, invalidate and alienate Esther. We are dealing with a chronic and barely visible trauma; a "microtraumatic" (Crastnopol, 2015) *condition*, we could say, rather than a punctual traumatic impact. This trauma, subtle and cumulative, divides Esther into a public version (subdued, disconnected from herself) and an internal version of herself, a repressed real self that, with the accidental injury to her leg, begins to manifest itself.

From here begins a particular descent into hell. Fascinated by the wound on her leg, Esther inflicts new injuries on herself. The story evolves along with the spiral of mutilation into which Esther plunges. Esther becomes obsessed with her own body and her ability to injure it (probably a last redoubt of freedom and self-determination). She cuts herself, rips off chunks of flesh and eats them or preserves them to eat later. In a chilling scene in which there is no sound other than that which comes from Esther herself, we see her open new wounds and drink the blood that flows from them.

Esther's mental fragmentation is presented to us with particular force in two scenes. At a working dinner, Esther has a hallucination in which she watches, terrified, as her own arm is severed from her body and left lying on the tablecloth, just another object next to the cutlery and plates. Esther is literally broken into disconnected pieces, and the film makes us part of this idea in a scene that is slow and anguished. Later, the film's most climactic sequence again has a split-screen format: in each half of the shot we observe partial actions of the protagonist (a hand grabbing something, a piece of her head moving to catch a sound, etc.) that occur at separate points in the story but are shown simultaneously. The scene literally presents us with a disjointed temporality. We hear the sound of voices and footsteps on the other side of Esther's hotel room door. This combination of elements conveys that, at this point, Esther has completely lost mental cohesion and contact with the outside world.

Post-traumatic fragmentations of identity (II): Dividing others to preserve them

The structural division of which we speak not only affects the sense of self, but also applies to the image that the subject has of others. This, as an effect of trauma, can also become fragmented. For the child abused at the hands of a primary caregiver or a referential figure (for example, a parent or a teacher), the adult is someone who protects and gives affection and, simultaneously, someone who provokes incomprehensible terror and pain. How can this contradiction be resolved? This is often accompanied by severe disturbances in communication stemming from the adult (Beebe & Lachman, 2014; Lyons-Ruth, Bronfman, & Parsons, 1999), or a disorganization of the adult's caregiving strategies (for example, an oscillation between hostile and helpless states of mind towards – or in the face of – the child) (Solomon & George, 2011). The incongruence to which the victim is exposed (we also find it in cases of intimate partner violence, for example) is very difficult to assimilate, it forces the person to see the other as a non-cohesive solution of different others (see also Liotti, 2004). The paradox that the aggressor is the one who has the power to calm the victim's anguish and pain makes it impossible to answer some questions that we all implicitly ask ourselves when we are in a relationship: *Will I be understood, helped, saved? Am I recognized and loved? Who am I for the other?* The victim's inability to resolve this interpersonal conundrum forces their mind to resort to another dissociative solution: the other is perceived as an incoherent sum of versions, fragments that provoke opposing emotions (Liotti, 2004).

Spider (Cronenberg, 2002) offers a powerful cinematic expression of this phenomenon. The story introduces us to Dennis, a schizophrenic patient who, recently discharged from hospital, returns to the neighborhood where he spent his childhood. The film takes us through Dennis' early memories, where the main protagonist is a sweet and protective mother, repeatedly abused and betrayed by an alcoholic, aggressive, and adulterous father. Between father and mother is the character of Yvonne, a prostitute who frequents the bar that the father sneaks out to every night to get drunk, and whom he repeatedly sleeps with. Yvonne's character, portrayed as an obscene and ugly (almost monstrous) woman, threatens to break into the family's domestic life and shatter the protective bubble in which Dennis and his sweet mother live. In one of the film's most dramatic moments, Dennis' father and Yvonne conspire against the mother, murder her, and bury her. Thus, the prostitute gets to live in the house: the home has been invaded by the monster. The film immerses us in Dennis' psychotic vision. Consequently, we do not discover until the end of the story that the figures of the angelic mother and the monstrous whore are, in fact, the same person. Dennis, traumatized by a toxic family relationship and unable to reconcile the contradictory aspects of his relationship with a mother who hurt him, divided her image into two split representations (one idealized, the other devalued). For years, his mind strove to keep these representations isolated from each other. The final revelation is accompanied in the film by another discovery: unable to tolerate what he experienced as his mother's betrayal, it was little Dennis who murdered his parents one night by leaving the gas tap on. As with other Cronenberg films, *Spider* powerfully depicts the distortions of memory, the mechanisms of mass repression, and the internal divisions of the mind, all of which are linked to trauma.

Figure 2.2 In *Spider* (Cronenberg, 2002), Denis deals with relational pain and confusion by dividing the representation of his mother into two opposing images, as well as by obsessively creating web-like structures that help him keep his psychic balance.

Uninvited guests

Another relevant aspect of post-traumatic fragmentation, also present in horror films, concerns introjections. After a sufficient number of traumatic episodes, the aggressor may be inscribed in the mind of an individual as an internal presence, an internal structure or psychic subsystem with its own motivations and goals, not integrated into the rest of the personality (Eagle, 2018). Jay Frankel recovers Ferenzci's reflections on this phenomenon and interprets it in terms of an "identification with the aggressor:" the desperate operation of a psyche that, exposed to violence from which it is impossible to escape, ends up assuming the perspective that the aggressor has on it (2022). These considerations are in line with Fairbairn's theory of introjects resulting from interpersonal trauma (1952). For this author, repetitive aggressions or neglect, within relationships with adults (specifically those who are referential or attachment figures), expose the child to a series of overwhelming affects (pain, fear, anger, despair) against which their vulnerable mind needs to defend itself. Again, the meaninglessness of being harmed by figures who themselves have a caregiving role (and the unbearable unpredictability that comes from being exposed to danger within a presumed protective relationship) require the child's mind to perform some kind of defensive operation (even if this comes at the cost of distortion). This operation consists, according to Fairbairn, in *introjecting* the bad objects from outside (the aggressive, rejecting, inconsistent figures), and identifying with them. The evil received by the child in the form of aggression or rejection becomes experienced as an endogenous evil, a characteristic of the self. For the child, being able to say to himself "there is something essentially negative in me that causes this maltreatment" offers the security of living in a more ordered world than saying "there is something essentially disordered, unpredictable and dangerous out there, and I can do nothing to control it" (Fairbairn, 1952b, p.66). Fairbairn's famous quote that "It is better to be a sinner in a world ruled by God than to live in a world ruled by the Devil" emphasizes this essential need for meaning and order.

The bad object, incorporated within the psyche in the form of an introject, becomes persecutory, punishing, and prone to sabotage all forms of well-being: victims are likely to feel unworthy and alienated, doomed to unhappiness (Monk, 2023), or very likely to reject, withdraw from, or obstruct the positive opportunities that life sometimes presents them with. Fairbairn suggests that the introjection of the bad object, in addition, confers a double fantasy on the victim: 1. From the inside, this object becomes more controllable; 2. The person is sure that, if he or she manages to develop acceptable behavior (if he or she ever manages to be good), the introjected object may be satisfied and stop exerting its punishment. Although these fantasies are very destructive to people's identity and self-esteem, it is important to understand that they bring with them an enormous secondary benefit: they order the world and limit the unbearable meaninglessness of trauma. In Janoff-Bulman's terms, they restore some hope that basic assumptions about order, justice, and causality are not entirely and irreversibly fractured (1992).

Subjectively, introjects function as "evoked partners" (D. Stern, 1985) with a harmful, critical, or exploitative character. Critchfield and Benjamin have described some ways in which these "copies" can exert their influence on the subjective life of the victim: making the victim behave towards others as the perpetrator did towards them; behaving as if the caregiver were present; treating themselves as the perpetrator treated them (2008).

Robert Wise used a novel by Shirley Jackson (*The Haunting of Hill House* [1959]) to explore these questions in his film *The Haunting* (1963). Its protagonist, Eleanor, has spent half her life in a toxic relationship with a disabled and possessive mother who has been under her care for years. After her mother's death, Eleanor is able to return to a normal life of freedom and, perhaps, enjoyment. She is then summoned by a scientist who wishes to investigate the alleged paranormal events that have taken place in an old mansion, with the help of several people who are potentially sensitive to such phenomena. In the house, Eleanor and her companions witness some of these manifestations, which the protagonist interprets in a personal way. The knocks heard in the night or the messages that inexplicably appear on the walls seem to be calls addressed to her: is it her dead mother, irritated by Eleanor's awakening to a new life? Introjective mechanisms combine with projective ones, in a dynamic that dissolves the boundaries between the internal and the external: the voice of the aggressive mother has been incorporated into Eleanor's fragile psyche, and is now perceived externally, in the form of a supernatural threat.

As the story progresses, loyalty to the internal object attacks any chance Eleanor has of acquiring mental autonomy. Despite the efforts of her companions to get her to leave, Eleanor is certain that she cannot, *must* not, separate herself from the mansion-mother. Unable to resolve the conflict between the split aspects of her mind (her longings for personal development on the one hand, her identification with the aggressor on the other), Eleanor crashes her car and dies in the grounds of the house, in a final act of bonding with the mother she could never leave behind.

Psycho also reflects on the power of identification with the aggressor and the effect of traumatic introjects on mental functioning (Hitchcock, 1960). Norman Bates, after a childhood subjected to a fusional, toxic, and domination-based relationship with a very fragile mother, and unprotected as a result of an isolated life and the absence of his father, has incorporated the internal voice of the mother into his subjective experience. She functions as a progressively stronger presence within him, to the point that Norman's desire and will are displaced by the introject, making Norman murder the women to whom he is originally attracted.

A third example of this phenomenology, as explored by horror cinema, appears in the recent *Talk to Me* (Philippou & Philippou, 2022). Mia, the protagonist of this film, is persuaded by the ghost of her mother (who had committed suicide in front of her eyes when she was a child) that she must murder her little brother Riley in order to "free" him. The story told in this film is that of an internal conflict that plays out within the mind of this young girl, between resolution in order to resume individual development, and remaining loyal to the figure of this ambiguous and mysterious mother whom she cannot "save" from suicide. In this film, the ghost (as in *The Haunting* [Wise, 1963]) corresponds to an internal object that, as an effect of a relationship overloaded with toxicity or ambiguity, has acquired the properties of a persecutory object, an aggressor that boycotts opportunities for development or stimulates self-destructive patterns of behavior. Towards the end of the story, Mia is on the verge of obeying her introjected mother's command and murdering Riley by driving him in a wheelchair towards a busy road, but she finally manages to resist her mother's voice and it is she who is thrown into the flow of traffic.

As has been suggested above, traumatic contents, despite being relegated to an obscure region of the mind, do not cease to be active and never lose their capacity to burst into awareness when they are least expected. These irruptions of unprocessed experiences have, for the victim, a persecutory character: the impression of a threat that insists on presenting itself, and against which it is very difficult to protect oneself. The adversaries of horror films (i.e., the ghost, the monster, the voices that echo in the house at night) are often representatives of a traumatic past that has not been adequately registered, witnessed, or spoken. The anomalous inscription of these wounds is precisely what turns them into 'phantasmagorical' material: something halfway between the internal and the external, between the real and the fantasized, that keeps coming back. In the following pages, we concentrate on the re-emergence of traumatic contents, and on the explorations that horror narrative has made of this phenomenon: the return (often camouflaged by a supernatural appearance) of trauma.

Chapter 3

Modes of traumatic re-emergence in modern horror cinema

At the beginning of *The Fog* (Carpenter, 1980), the Californian town of Antonio Bay prepares to celebrate the centenary of its founding. A century ago, after a horrific shipwreck off its shores, the scattered inhabitants of the region coalesced into a community that today remembers its history and celebrates itself.

But order begins to dissolve, slowly and subtly, in Antonio Bay. It begins with a brick falling from the wall of the sacristy where one of the protagonists (Father Malone) drinks, revealing the diary of his grandfather, one of the town's first inhabitants. It continues with strange blackouts in different areas of the town, car alarms going off spontaneously, or the hydraulic platforms of the mechanic's workshop starting up without anyone pressing the switch. Most disturbing of all, however, is a glowing fog that, like a huge hand, arrives unexpectedly from the sea (had the weather forecast not assured that they would enjoy a pristine sky during the festivities?) and creeps into the town, blinding the streets.

As if that were not enough, on the morning of the day set for the celebrations, the body of a crew member is found inside a fishing boat. The sailor has all the signs of having been at the bottom of the sea for months: there is mud under his fingernails, his lungs are waterlogged, his skin is swollen. But how can this be, when another of the protagonists in this story swears that he was with the victim less than two days ago? No one can account for what is happening, and all are limited in their ability to perceive the unknown threat that hovers over the village and, like the fog, lacks a definite form. These manifestations are the "sightings" (Clute, 2006) of a subterranean truth that peeks through to the surface, provoking the anticipation of a still uncertain danger.

Later, Father Malone reads the diary found in the wall, and with it we discover the origin of these strange 'symptoms' that were announced the day before. A hundred years ago, a group of lepers, who had been isolated from their own island, sought refuge on the coast. The leader of this group had agreed with the shore dwellers that, in exchange for part of their fortune, they would be granted a piece of land to live on. However, the landmen took advantage of a fog that had risen that night to light fires, which misdirected the ship and caused it to be wrecked upon the rocks. Thanks to the stolen fortune and the hidden crime, the community of Antonio Bay bloomed.

DOI: 10.4324/9781003468981-4

But today, the fog from a century ago has risen again, and within it travel the drowned. With their rotting bodies and their navigation tools, they roam the streets and knock on doors; they seek to be seen and recognized. Above all, they seek compensation in blood.

Like so many other films of the genre, *The Fog* is a tale of injustice and punishment. But it is also a story that, with the metaphorical language of terror, speaks of trauma and its manifestations. Traumas do not belong only to the victims; sometimes they also affect those who inflict harm on others (as the psychology of the ex-soldier, among others, has shown us). In the subsoil of Antonio Bay's conscience lies an unexpiated crime and, with it, an unresolved guilt that will fall with special force on the descendant of one of the perpetrators: Father Malone.

The motif of the fog, so well employed by Carpenter in his film, symbolically illustrates the way in which the traumatic past, despite having been relegated to watertight, hidden compartments of the mind, *re-emerges*. The fog is an object that cannot be contained, has no defined borders, and constantly changes shape by virtue of this liminal state, halfway between solid and liquid. This is reminiscent of the distress felt by some post-traumatic syndrome patients: it appears as disturbances that are disconnected from the present ("Why do I feel this just now?"), as a generalized anguish ("I feel irritable, restless, unable to sleep, agitated... but why?"), or as the anxious anticipation of a danger that seems to infiltrate a variety of situations, despite the world around them trying to make the patient see reason ("Everything is going to be fine, there is nothing to fear"). Sightings within horror films, as we will detail below, move in a similar register to that of many symptoms of post-traumatic stress: a threat looms above the person, without yet having a defined form.

One of the key moments in the story told by Carpenter in *The Fog* is a meeting in which several characters, having read the newly discovered diary, discuss the course they should take. Father Malone is convinced that a fatal threat looms over the small town, and that it will not go away until the dead are appeased and the guilt is atoned for. This means that the celebrations must be cancelled. Against this stance, the mayor's willingness to hold out for a few more hours and allow the town to enjoy the festivities, in which so much hope and money has been invested, rises up. Carpenter (like so many storytellers in the genre) confronts us with the conflict between processing the trauma and ignoring it, between attempting to heal it or denying the wound.

And here, again, a bridge is built that connects us to the phenomenology of trauma. Herman suggests that the conflict between the will to deny horrible events and the will to proclaim them out loud is the central dialectic of psychological trauma (2015). If in the previous chapter we described the efforts of the traumatized mind to fragment itself and isolate the trauma from the rest of the contents of the self, it is no less true that such a conspiracy of silence within the mind is only one side of the coin. On the other side is the psyche's need to connect with what happened in order to reprocess the damage and reintegrate the "foreign body" of the traumatic into the sense of self. The traumatized mind struggles between silence and speech, as Richman points out: "[...] at the same time as there is a tendency to deny or hide the horrors, there is an imperative to speak the truth" (2006, p. 641). Herman adds that this conflict transcends the realm of the individual to penetrate societies and cultures. In the public sphere, all of us (victims, perpetrators, and witnesses) are confronted with the choice between telling and keeping silent. Those who listen to testimonies of sexual abuse, humiliation, or physical abuse of the most vulnerable are compelled to respond either with testimony or silence: "[...] when traumatic events are of human design, those who bear witness are caught in the conflict between victim [who wants to speak] and perpetrator [who wants silence]. It is morally impossible to remain neutral in this conflict. The bystander is forced to take sides" (2015, p. 7).

When silence or defenses gain the upper hand in this dialectic, secrecy prevails. The individual's life unfolds under an apparent absence of pain, a denial of what happened that can vary in extent: from those who have forgotten everything to those who remember the events but feel nothing about them. The scientific literature abounds in descriptions of victims who are affectively numbed, and of the emotional anesthesia that immunizes them from the emotions linked to the trauma and, in the most serious cases, from affectivity in general (Lanius, Vermetten, & Pain, 2010).

However, trauma tends to re-emerge, under different 'masks': that of the physical symptom, the flashback, the recurrent dream, among others. The traumatized subject experiences the intrusion of memories, sensations, or emotions linked to the trauma at the most unexpected moments and in the face of stimuli apparently unrelated to the original trauma. While bathing their children, or when buying the newspaper, or when innocently falling asleep against the bus window, the victim is suddenly assaulted by intrusive noises, images, smells, sounds, bodily sensations, or thoughts that bring them back to the traumatic experience and put their body in a state of alert. Fear, humiliation, anger, and other unresolved emotions creep in, like Antonio Bay's fog, to the very corners of the psychic life.

On other occasions, the re-emergence of trauma may take the form of a state of affective or interpersonal disorganization: the subject is overwhelmed by abrupt, unexpected emotional states, interacts in oscillating and contradictory ways with significant others, or experiences a significant loss of ego cohesion, for example. These phenomena can be seen as the result of attachment defensive patterns reaching their functional limit (Liotti, 2011). Attachment reorganization patterns based on the avoidance of intimacy, dominating others through coercive or seductive attitudes, using sex as a weapon, compulsively caring for others, or isolating oneself through schizoid functioning, among others, are overtaken at some point by levels of emotional intensity or intimacy that exceed the defensive effectiveness of these strategies (Crittenden, 2016; Lyons-Ruth & Jacobvitz, 2016). Subjective states associated with attachment trauma then resurface, provoking a loss of control over one's own mind and behavior.

Such episodes of disorganization may occur, for example, when a developmental transition or a relevant change in the person's life increases the intensity of those contents that the mind strives to isolate. One female patient, accustomed for years to remaining cordially distant in her social relationships (always far from an intimacy she anticipated as overwhelming), began to experience strong anxiety symptoms and a compulsion to binge eating with the birth of her first child. This transition had caused her defensive program to cease to function, making the feelings of intimacy and dependence (hitherto dissociated) to become too intense. In addition, as was soon discovered in therapy, motherhood reactivated in this woman the hitherto dissociated pain of a neglected childhood. This woman asked for help after finding herself, on more than one occasion, very close to mistreating her baby when he became particularly demanding.

Disorganization can also occur when difficult experiences in the present, by accumulation or by a kind of retroactive influence (Breuer & S. Freud, 1895), bring back the emotions and pain of unprocessed early trauma. After being exposed to a harsh public reprimand by his new boss, a man developed agoraphobia that prevented him from leaving the house and, logically, from going to work. The biographical exploration of this patient revealed a history in which he had been subtly but repeatedly humiliated by an older brother. This humiliation usually took place at home and in front of other siblings and their parents, who, as the patient recalled, seemed to enjoy the older brother's perverse game. The public scorn experienced at work added to a historical experience of humiliations and re-signified them negatively (i.e. confirming for this man that the social world is dangerous or that he is always exposed to humiliation).

Intense stress, fatigue, or the accumulation of social adversities (as may be experienced by people belonging to minority or stigmatized groups, or in multi-stressed families, for example) are also potential triggers of disorganization. It is not uncommon to observe that people burdened by poverty, chronic threat, or lack of support in their environment, often engage in affective reactions that, from an external perspective, appear disproportionate and (self-)destructive.

But disorganization does not only come from markedly painful or relatively large-scale events, such as those we have reviewed so far. A mere change in interpersonal balance can have a disorganizing effect on people with insecure or traumatic attachment histories. And so, small separations (for example, a brief work trip by a partner), a harmless misunderstanding (for example, the person tries to contact a friend who does not answer their call), or the beginning of a new and promising emotional relationship can initiate a cascade of distress and internal fragmentation. The common denominator of these situations is that they activate the attachment system, which, as we know, for some people may have been strongly associated with disorganization:

> Adult survivors of childhood abuse and early attachment disorganization can lead lives that are not considered abnormal or pathological, either subjectively or by standard psychiatric diagnostic criteria, until their control strategy is forcibly suspended under the influence of a powerful stressor that activates the attachment system.
>
> (Liotti, 2011, p. 390)

If there is a fundamental common ground between traumatic phenomenology and the horror narrative, it is probably that of *repetition*. Horror stories almost always begin with the aforementioned sightings that hint at the presence of impending danger: a kitchen where cupboards open spontaneously and without explanation; a human body on which inexplicable marks begin to appear; noises circulating around the house that sound suspiciously like the whisper of a human voice trying to send a message. Later in the story, the sightings become established as an undeniable threat that the character (however much he may wish to avoid it) must confront. A "thickening" (Clute, 2006) of the narrative conflict ensues: the monster becomes real and acquires form. This is analogous to the appearance, in patients, of specific post-traumatic symptoms (for example, flashbacks, repetitive dreams, intrusive thoughts, etc.), the content of which refers directly to the traumatic event. Post-traumatic symptoms, like the horror genre, tell us an essential human story: that of something that, despite our resistance, insists on returning.

There is something *monstrous* about the way these post-traumatic manifestations take over people's lives. Like the monster (or any supernatural threat depicted in the horror narrative), the re-enactment of the trauma in memory, intimate relationships, dreams, etc., has a sense of "exteriority" that violently bursts into people's lives. Traumatic re-experiencing is played out in the borderline between the external aspect of the symptom (which is experienced as something alien) and its internal origin.

And, as happens with those symptoms suffered by the patient, in horror films the characters exposed to the attack of the monster or the ghost sense that this threat, anomalous and foreign, has something to do with them, that it *says* something about them.

Trauma exposes us to that terrible paradox: something overwhelms us from within, but does not feel as though it belongs to us. There is a piece of the past that, instead of being accessed and processed by the subject as something of their own, is imposed on them as a 'de-subjectivized' reality, an intrusion. Trauma retains its pure perceptual quality: untouched by the reflections or words that would allow it to be integrated into identity, it remains a concrete, hyper-real element that repeatedly and violently bursts into subjective life. After trauma, we are passive objects of a mental state.

This problem has been thematized by horror cinema as an invasion of the supernatural into the character's life. The monster, despite its connection to the characters' past or to the community in which they live, is not recognized by them, it is an uninvited visitor. Its excessiveness derives in part from its belonging to the plane of the dissociated and the unrecognized. When they reappear, these contents are presented to the mind as something far removed from its usual codes of interpretation, bizarre and illegible.

There are many films that demonstrate that horror has, at its narrative core, an interest in the re-emergence of trauma. In *The Exorcist* (Friedkin, 1973), the unresolved grief of Father Karras resurfaces when a girl possessed by the devil addresses him in the voice of her dead mother. In *His House* (Weekes, 2020), strange presences move behind the walls, bringing with them the memory of a traumatic migration story suffered by its protagonists. In *The Others* (Amenábar, 2001), the ghostly presences that terrorize the protagonist's mother and children force

Figure 3.1 In *His House* (Weekes, 2020), strange presences move behind the walls, bringing with them the memory of a traumatic migration story suffered by its protagonists.

the recognition of a forgotten atrocity. Unresolved loss and hatred insist on being present through a monster that visits the widowed mother and son in *The Babadook* (Kent, 2014). In these and other examples, horror is presented to us as a narrative about memory and repetition. These films teach us that some memories, rather than being recovered, are *imposed*.

Under the effect of re-emergence, one of the central features of the traumatic experience, discussed in previous sections, is actualized: the impression that what has been experienced is illegible, impossible to think about or name. The network of words and representations that we share and use to account for reality proves useless when it comes to expressing the experiences of those who are assaulted by the sensations, mental images, or compulsive actions associated with a trauma. Expressed in Lacanian terms, the emergence of trauma involves the irruption of an excessive Real in people's lives. This Real is a surplus of stimulation, incomprehensible and inexpressible, which violently tears the symbolic fabric and condemns us to the loss of our narrative competence (Aznar Alarcón & Varela Feal, 2019) or to silence.

Brain hijacking: The tyranny of the limbic system

The aforementioned resistance of traumatic memories to being controlled, their capacity to return in the form of a hyper-real version of the trauma, and their inaccessibility to language, are characteristics with a well-studied neurological basis. Research with post-traumatic stress disorder (PTSD) patients reveals that the brains of these subjects, when they remember their traumas, show a very particular pattern of activation: the activity of the brain areas in charge of detecting danger, making us feel fear, and activating attack–flight survival responses is disproportionately high. More specifically, this translates into an asymmetry that is recurrently observed in scanner tests: the limbic areas of the brain are over-activated, while there is reduced activity in the prefrontal area (van der Kolk, 2015).

The limbic area is the seat of our most primary emotional system, the place where our survival-related emotions are produced. It is a brain region that we share with all mammals and which – as its name suggests – is located on the boundary or "limbus" between the reptilian brain (the deepest layer of the brain) and the neocortex (the most superficial layer). Within the limbic system, the amygdala functions as a kind of "smoke detector" (van der Kolk, 2015) that quickly and automatically assesses what is painful or threatening, and triggers very rapid responses in preparation for attack or flight.[1] Increased heart rate, hyperventilation, increased muscle tension, etc., are all part of this amygdala survival plan. In addition, of course, to the behavior it triggers to save us: for example, jumping to protect us from a snake's bite. Because the amygdala processes sensory information faster than the prefrontal brain, it decides whether situations pose a threat to our survival even before we are aware of the danger. By the time we realize what is happening, our body has probably already reacted.

Pain without language: Narrative collapse and muteness

What has been described in previous sections regarding anomalies in the recording of traumatic memories (a memory that is pure presence and disjointed emotion) is accompanied, during the reemergence of these memories, by another very particular alteration. The traumatic memory does not allow itself to be organized as a story, a comprehensible and communicable narrative. These memories, far from having a format of approach-node-denouement, are fragmentary displays of an experience, a sum of loose pieces of very intense sensory information. Traumatic memory, in addition to being hijacked by intense emotions, suffers from narrative collapse.

This phenomenon also appears to be based on a number of neural abnormalities. When remembering trauma, the brains of PTSD patients show asymmetrical activation patterns, favoring the right hemisphere. While this hemisphere processes the emotional and sensory aspects of the experience, the left hemisphere specializes in verbal and linguistic processing of the experience. The right hemisphere *senses* what has happened, storing the overall sensation and affective tone of the memory; the left hemisphere orders and *recounts* what has happened, contextualizing the memory and constructing its meaning. Under normal circumstances, the interhemispheric conversation allows our knowledge of the past to contain a balance between the visceral aspects of the experience and a reflection on it. As a result, it is the person who owns their memory, not the other way around. For the traumatized brain, however, this bridge is severely weakened, causing traumatic recall to take the form of emotional intrusion that resists being put into words (van der Kolk, 2015). Other differences that have been found in brain connectivity between PTSD and comparison subjects point to the nonverbal nature of traumatic memory recall in PTSD subjects (Lanius et al., 2004; Rauch, Shin, & Phelps, 2006).

The hijacked brain described in the last section is not only an organ on alert, overwhelmed by unbearable emotion, it is also a *muted* brain.

> All trauma is preverbal [...] Even years later traumatized people often have enormous difficulty telling other people what has happened to them. Their bodies reexperience terror, rage, and helplessness, as well as the impulse to fight or flee, but these feelings are almost impossible to articulate.
> (van der Kolk, 2015, pp. 125–126)

Finally, the massive secretion of stress hormones has a particular impact on the hippocampus, a part of our brain responsible for the consolidation of conscious autobiographical memories (McEwen, 2007). With the hippocampus we transform a raw experience into an organized, comprehensible, and communicable mental scene. When, in the course of a high-impact experience, these hormones begin to fall on the hippocampus in massive doses, this organ is initially over-stimulated and, a little later, de-stimulated.

The initial overstimulation of the hippocampus causes some traumatic impressions to be burned in. The result is the generation of some 'flashbulb memories,' those very clear and sensorially powerful mnemonic impressions that some patients cannot help but see with terrifying clarity on the screen of their consciousness. But as the stress continues, adrenaline eventually devastates the hippocampus' ability to articulate the sensations into an integrated and comprehensible memory.

Traumatic memories are stored in the form of somatic sensations, visual images, and auditory traces in the amygdala, instead of being integrated through the mediation of the hippocampus and the prefrontal cortex. Linguistic memory – the result of conversation between the two hemispheres of the brain, activity in Broca's area, and integration at the hippocampal level – is disabled during trauma. As a result, sensory, affective, and motor memories are often divorced from conscious awareness and symbolic understanding.

It has been observed that one of the common reactions after traumatic events is the inability to talk about what happened. Victims of sexual assault or abuse, for example, often relate the trauma as a succession of scattered elements: words spoken by the offender or the victim, a painful sensation in the body, the perception of an approaching silhouette, smells and sounds. Unlike normal memory, traumatic memory lacks cohesion. This does not mean that victims do not remember the specific scenes of the trauma or cannot refer to them ("the man appeared in the street and assaulted me"), but that the sensory–emotional component is often invasive and disabling. There is a kind of decoupling between what one knows about the danger and pain one has experienced, and what one can explain or *say* about it. This excess of the emotional over the verbal invalidates much of the victims' attempts to contain, reduce, or communicate their suffering (Brewin, Dalgleish, & Joseph, 1996; Ehlers & Clark, 2000).

This is a variation on the theme developed in the previous chapter: the dismantling of our symbolic capacity at the hands of a violent and invasive Real. Faced with the hyper-real blow of trauma, words cease to serve us. Although some people can talk about their past traumas (even describing in detail the damage that was inflicted, in some cases), their stories rarely capture the inner truth of the experience:

> It is enormously difficult to organize one's traumatic experiences into a coherent account – a narrative with a beginning, a middle, and an end [...]. When words fail, haunting images capture the experience and return as nightmares and flashbacks.
>
> (van der Kolk, 2015, pp. 125–126)

Carol, the protagonist of *Repulsion* (Polanski, 1963), is assaulted by terrible flashbacks of a rape she suffered as a child. In a memory that she experiences as real (and, with Carol, so do we), an anonymous assailant enters the house where she is alone and tries to rape her. During these scenes, we see her screaming, writhing, trying to escape from the assailant. Their bodies hit the furniture and struggle over the messy sheets. However, there is an anomaly: we hear nothing. It is a silent scene. Carol's mouth, open in a scream, emits no sound. The violence of the bodies does not sound either. In the mind of this victim, there is no sound because there are no words or meanings with which to approach the trauma and reduce it. Trauma is a communicative desert that makes it impossible to say anything to oneself or to others, something Polanski portrayed in this extremely painful scene repeated several times throughout the film, marked by a perfect silence interrupted only by the ticking of a clock.

Horror is perhaps the genre closest to the representation of muteness. As we have developed above, these films are full of moments analogous to trauma, in which a surplus of external stimulation (for example, the sight of the ghost, the chase of the monster, the murderer opening the door) becomes incomprehensible and unbearable. The scream is probably the other side of this same coin that is symbolic inability. Faced with the supernatural excess that threatens them, the characters in horror stories are often reduced to mutism or screaming. We spectators, on the other hand, resonate with this when we scream in a movie theatre or remain frozen during the terrifying narration we hear around the campfire. In the absence of reason and discourse, the only thing left is to be silent or to scream.

Inhabiting an alternative language

Faced with the inability to understand and speak imposed by trauma, the minds of some victims in films can resort to the creation of an alternative symbolic universe, a kind of 'neo-language' that allows them to preserve a glimmer of psychic equilibrium.

This is what we see in *Spider* (Cronenberg, 2002). The protagonist, a schizophrenic man assaulted by memories of the domestic violence he experienced during his childhood, compulsively fills his notebooks with tiny handwriting, accompanied by a mechanical, inaudible, unintelligible speech. These desperate strategies with which the character tries to reassemble himself or to preserve a certain mental composure are also materialized in a ritual: he crosses his room with a rope that runs from one wall to another and creates a kind of supporting web, similar to a spider's web (which gives the film its title). *Art brut* (raw art), made famous by some psychotic patients, obeys a very similar logic: the paper is filled with tiny symbols, faces, lines that divide the surface and seem to support a kind of fragile structure, strokes that resemble letters and that seem to be determined (but incapable) of saying the most important thing. Jean Dubuffet and Robert Tatin are the most famous exponents of this artistic vocation, which comes out of stories of great damage and mental fragility, and which aspires to a certain form of psychic reorganization.

Saint Maud (Glass, 2019) is another film interested in the psychotic production of an alternative language. Katie, a nurse traumatized by a dark episode in her previous hospital job, seeks solace in a religious conversion, which leads her to adopt the name of a saint: Maud. In her new life, she is hired to provide home care for Amanda, a terminally ill cancer patient who spends her last weeks of life partying and having sex with prostitutes. Maud sees her new job as a God-given mission to save Amanda's soul. She sets about trying to straighten out her life, which ends catastrophically and humiliatingly for her. This represents a sort of final blow to her fragile mental balance. The framework provided by her religious experience has been violated by a woman who mocks her beliefs, and Maud's sense of control begins to crack; she is in increasing danger of becoming Katie again and reconnecting with an unbearably traumatic past.

As Maud descends into the spiral of post-traumatic delirium, she loses her connection to reality and, particularly, her contact with the symbolic. This process culminates in the development of an idiosyncratic language, through which God and she converse about her mission. This language takes the form of psychotic gibberish, a kind of divine voice that only Maud is able to hear and decipher. Another manifestation of this symbolic dismantling is seen in a scene late in the film, in which Maud is visited by Joy, a former colleague from her work at the hospital. Joy talks persistently to Maud in an attempt to reconcile with her and to pull her out of the mental quagmire into which she is sinking. Meanwhile, Maud/Katie stands with her back turned, mute, and gazes at the clouds through the window with a beatific expression: she believes she sees in them a divine message containing instructions on the steps she must take. The post-traumatic break with reality unfolds, in this scene, as the impossibility of communicating in a common, shared language.

We will see in Chapter 4 that, although trauma attacks language and threatens to leave characters anchored to alienated modes of expression such as those we have just illustrated, there is an alternative. Some films show us the possibility of a middle way, often facilitated by the figure of a medium or a shaman or a rite that allows us to enter into a new language. This language helps to *express the inexpressible* without losing contact with reality. It provides a sort of symbolic 'knotting' that helps bring raw emotions and pain belonging to the Real into a new Symbolic that may be able to express something about the trauma. In horror films, the shaman is the one who can name the threat, tell the story of the monster, or share his own (traumatic) story of contact with the monster. Thus, he mediates the passage to a place where the traumatic lends itself to a certain kind of reordering or integration.

Caught in the primary process

In many horror movies, characters discover that they cannot rely on the support of the symbolic to face a threat: science fails to explain what is happening; institutions are powerless and incapable of containing the danger; words do not help the protagonist communicate what is happening. Speculating explanations about the fantastic excess presented on the screen (the threat the characters in the narrative face) is almost always a futile act, as the irruption of the Real precisely invalidates the symbolic.

Regarding the already described scene from *The Changeling* (Medak, 1980) in which the protagonist sees the ball that belonged to his dead daughter descend the staircase, a ball he threw into the river minutes before, Roas asserts: "To claim that the cause of the ball's appearance is the ghost of the dead child serves no purpose, since such a justification also goes beyond our idea of what is possible, of what is comprehensible" (2016, p. 58).

In the primary process, more typical of the childish mentality and the unconscious, the laws of chronology do not apply, so what was in the past can continue to be in the now, in an experience analogous to the "sacred time" that Mircea Eliade spoke of (and to which we will return) (1964). When the mind interprets reality from the primary process, history ceases to have the form of a forward-moving line and configures itself as a spiral that moves back and forth from the present to the past, equating these two temporal registers into a unique experience. Some moments are immortalized in memory, moments that do not undergo the natural transformation of mental contents. Thus, a mental landscape of frozen, repetitive moments arises.

The laws of logic do not apply either, so what was feared/desired/fantasized can be experienced as something that actually happened, in a confusion between the internal and the external. Here we have another abolition of the differentiating keys of rational thought: fantasy is confused with reality. In the geographies of the primary process, the child struck by misfortune feels responsible for it: the abuse received, the death of a loved one, the dissolution of the family, among other things, are experienced as the result of a magical power the child has over the world, something that they must have caused.

Although the primary process is especially associated with children's magical thinking, it is not an operation that we definitively leave behind as we grow up. On the contrary, it is something like an undercurrent of mental operations that continues to occur and, in the territory of the traumatic, gains special relevance. Years after the trauma, every time a rape victim goes to bed and starts to fall asleep, she feels that it is going to happen again (chronological time is annulled). The man who lost his wife due to an illness, despite his rational abilities, experiences a deep feeling of responsibility in a region of his psyche: he knows that, in some way, his wife's death was his fault, whether it be through his negligence or his inability to protect her or to detect the danger in time (the logical and rational discrimination of cause and effect are annulled).

The presence of the primary process in horror films (and its special link to traumatic processes) is particularly evident in two aspects: the alteration of the temporal order, on the one hand, and the failure of the principle of contradiction, on the other.

Disjointed time

The anomalous temporality of trauma has in horror fiction one of its best representatives. Horror stories abound in alterations of the flow of time. Time slows down, is paralyzed or develops in parallel to ordinary time. The protagonists are immersed in scenes where the difference between past and present disappears, and the borders of memory are suspended to let trauma (disguised as ghost) break through. The borders between dream and wakefulness, fantasy and logic, drive and thought are also suspended.

In all these cases, the ordering and calming effect of reason seems to be suspended too. The protagonist of the story (as well as the mind of trauma victims) is exposed to the irruption of raw emotional contents. The intrapsychic violence of post-traumatic phenomena is that of the irruption of emotion without the help of reason; or that of a regression into the past without a grip on the present. For victims of early trauma – such as maltreatment or child sexual abuse – this internal violence can also take the form of a re-immersion in childhood experience (i.e., helplessness, loneliness, and fear) without recourse to metaphor (i.e., the ability to compare past and present).

In one of the most powerful scenes of *A Nightmare on Elm Street* (Craven, 1984), we see Nancy locked in her parents' house, pursued by the supernatural killer Freddy Krueger. Nancy calls for help from her father, who is across the street, but he does not hear his daughter's screams. The door of the house has been locked by Nancy's mother, and the windows are barred to protect them from outside dangers: it is impossible to get out. What the parents do not know is that the threat comes from inside. In fact, Krueger appears just as Nancy's mother has fallen asleep on the sofa, completely drunk. She is the bearer of unprocessed trauma: Krueger's past murders of children, and her own contribution to Krueger's death. Now that she sleeps, repression is suspended and the nightmare emerges outside to haunt her daughter, who has become an unwitting heir to the traumas of the previous generation. The scene seems to suggest that the locked house in which Krueger moves with homicidal freedom is a metaphor for the mother's mind, where the daughter has been imprisoned and tormented by a violence she is unable to comprehend. In this scene, the traumatic memory (of the mother) intersects and confuses with the present experience (of the daughter); the past of some (the parents' generation) with the present of others (the young people who are systematically harassed and murdered by Krueger in their dreams); dream with wakefulness. There is a dissolution of boundaries and differentiations. Particularly, there is a subversion of temporality. It is an allegorical moment (an issue we will return to in detail shortly) where the statutes and distinctions that normally allow us to define reality, orient ourselves within it, and maintain sanity are annulled. The suspension of the secondary process in favor of the primary process is the key to the scene just described. Krueger is a remnant of the parents' traumatic past and is *also* a persecutor in the children's present. He is a painful memory of the parents and *also* a being of flesh and blood who can appear, attack, kill. He is a visitor in dreams, but he is *also* a presence that wanders through reality. He is dead and *also* remains alive.

Contradiction and allegorical moment

As mentioned above, the effect of trauma also translates into an attack on the differentiating codes of the Freudian secondary process, with which we organize our experience of the world. The principle of non-contradiction is naturally associated with an ordering of experience based on binary discriminations, on which our symbolic mind works. We derive meaning from a system of oppositions and differences: past vs present; fantasy vs reality; inside vs outside; familiar vs strange; friend vs foe; etc. This, according to Lowenstein, is absent in the phenomenology of post-traumatic states (2005). Trauma escapes these logics based on the principle of contradiction. For the traumatized person, the familiar and known world is at the same time a dangerous or strange scenario. Significant others can be sources of love and care and at other times (often unpredictably and uncontrollably for the subject) become dangerous figures. Institutions and authorities also condense some of this contradiction: they are the only place to turn to for protection and, frequently, they are also the source of responses that – by omission – side with the aggressor. After trauma, the distinctions that underpin our identity and self-esteem may cease to be useful, and the self is left circulating between contradictory representations: feeling good and bad, worthy and unworthy, clean and dirty, capable and helpless, and so on.

In the field of early relational trauma, this fracturing of categories and distinctions can be particularly relevant, as it affects essential aspects of identity, representations of the interpersonal world and, ultimately, basic trust. Early exchanges between primary caregivers and the child are the main source of knowledge about the world. Parents transform the raw and unavailable affective contents (*beta elements* [Bion, 1962]) into ordered and meaningful experiences for the child, coherent thoughts and memories that can be used for conscious thinking (*alpha elements* [Bion, 1962]). Through a repetition of mirroring interactions (Fonagy, Gergely, & Jurist, 2018), the child's inner experiences are absorbed, metabolized, and transformed by the caregiver into manageable mental material. In this way, both the contents of one's own mind and the transactions that take place in the interpersonal space become comprehensible and reliable (Fonagy et al., 2019). The world (both internal and external) acquires an order within the parent–child communicative circuit, a circuit in which the aforementioned parental responses of mirroring, mind-mindedness (Meins et al., 2002), parental mentalization (Slade, 2005), narratives that allow for processing of the emotional impacts experienced by the child (Oppenheim & Koren-Karie, 2021), or acts of reverie that allow for metabolizing of the experience (Bion, 1962) are deployed.

Observing the interactions between traumatized/disorganized caregivers and their children, however, offers a very different picture. In contact with their children, vulnerable parents display contradictory affective signals. For example, in the face of a child's state of intense emotional distress, a disorganized caregiver may attempt to hold and comfort the child and simultaneously avert their eyes or adopt a threatening or mocking vocal tone, which not only increases the child's original distress, but leads to a state of confusion about the meaning of the communicative signals that are reaching them. These cross-modal mismatches (Beebe and Lachman, 2014) are a key component of interactions that progressively disorganize the child's attachment, paralleling the disorganization of the parent's mental state (Solomon and George, 2011). For children exposed to phenomena of this kind, interpersonal experience escapes categorization. In our example, the good intentions contained in the caregiver's approach are combined with some sort of threat or urgency, making it impossible for the child to 'locate' the caregiver, their mental state, or the meaning of their actions (it also becomes very difficult to predict what will happen next). Social cues, exchanges, and words lose their communicative value. Subjectively, the child may find it difficult to know whether they feel close or far away from the caregiver, whether they are comfortable or uncomfortable, whether the caregiver is making them feel accepted (because they are reaching out to hold them) or rejected (because, at the same time, they are actively avoiding eye contact). The contradictory, disorganized (Oppenheim & Koren-Karie, 2021), or double-binding narratives that dominate communication in trauma-affected families contribute, during the child's growth years, to this nuclear confusion.

Sometimes these phenomena take the form of a transmission of parental trauma "in negative" (Tisseron, 2007), i.e. through non-verbal means and in conditions of secrecy or the absence of a narrative that gives meaning to painful interactions. This absence prevents the child from understanding why some interactions at home are so difficult, why intimacy is sometimes so uncomfortable, why or under what conditions parents dissociate, withdraw, explode aggressively, etc. What is transmitted is not a knowledge that can be elaborated or subject to symbolization, but an affective imprint without a signifier to anchor it, and that is therefore very difficult to connect and integrate with other experiences. Traumatized parents who have not processed (or even remembered) their trauma may display confused and very threatening responses, but, as already stated, in the absence of a narrative. The parent transmits to their child a harm that they cannot *talk* about, the child receives a harm that cannot be *named* and, perhaps, the children of subsequent generations will experience a harm that cannot even be *thought* of (Tisseron, 2007). Epistemic distrust or freezing (Fonagy et al., 2019) may be a final consequence of these trajectories, where interpersonal communication is presented to the child as a source of contradiction and distress. In short, trauma not only attacks the basic assumptions that sustain our trust (Janoff-Bulman, 1992), but also our capacity to orient ourselves through cognitive categories that make the world comprehensible.

These and other conditions contribute to the logical failure that Lowenstein places at the heart of the post-traumatic experience (2005). The consequence, for this author, is that trauma only allows itself to be represented visually with an ambiguous and shocking aesthetic that insists on escaping categorization. In horror cinema, this ambiguity is condensed in what the author calls the "allegorical moment." The allegorical moment implies a rupture of the binary categories with which we rationally organize reality: dead–alive; beautiful–ugly; past–present; health–disease. Trauma and horror join hands over the abyss of contradiction.

The author exemplifies this principle with the final scene of *Deathdream* (Clark, 1974), where a son killed in Vietnam has returned from the dead to visit his mother and lead her through a cemetery to a grave he has dug for himself. The mother, unable to accept that her son is really dead, clings to him. But his skin has begun to decompose, revealing that the young man is indeed a corpse. The son crawls into the grave and begins to throw dirt over himself. The mother, after a few moments, yields and helps her son, herself throwing earth over the mangled body of her son, who finally extends his hand to her in a gesture of farewell. As the mother kisses her son's hand, a car explodes in the distance. The explosion illuminates the cemetery with a glow reminiscent of Vietnam detonations.

This moment is allegorical, according to the author, insofar as it brings together aspects of experience which, although contradictory, are all equally real and participate in a terrible simultaneity: the persistence of the son in the mother's life despite his death; the confluence of two spaces (America and Vietnam; the quiet locality and the country at war) which have become irreversibly intertwined; the simultaneity of horror, loss, and hope.

Horror films are full of allegorical moments. The encounter (and the final confrontation) with the monster almost always has the characteristics of something that is *impossible-but-is-happening*, an event that takes place "at the unpredictable and often painful juncture where past and present collide" (Lowenstein, 2005, p. 9).

In these scenes, the action circulates around a center of contradictions or ambiguities that do not end up being defined in a univocal representation. They can function, in this way, as a cinematographic manifestation of the traumatic Real. When they appear in the story, they do so as a kind of irruption, a shocking moment that, if you like, has the effects of a "narrative black hole:" meaning is swallowed up and, around it, our perception of the film is reorganized.

The scene in *Psycho* (Hitchcock, 1960) in which Lila Crane descends into the basement and discovers the corpse of Norman Bates' mother is perhaps one of the most popular allegorical moments in the history of the genre. Lila approaches the old woman, who is sitting under a naked light bulb. When she touches her shoulder, we discover that it is in fact the woman's corpse, an empty body preserved with the embalming techniques that her son Norman has mastered so well. At this terrifying sight Lila screams and holds her hands to her face. Behind her, in the doorway, a white-haired woman suddenly appears, raising a knife with the intention of murdering Lila (reminding us of the way in which, during the first act of the film, her sister Marion was killed in the famous shower scene). In a fast-moving sequence, our minds are confused: Norman's mother is dead, a body preserved in a chair, as we have just discovered. But she is not quite dead, because how else could she *also* be on the doorstep? The 'living' mother, the one approaching Lila with the knife held aloft, we discover is Norman himself, cross-dressing in her clothes and hair. Norman (who was raised under the control of this demanding, castrating mother) has melted into her. Instead of placing his dead mother in a symbolic place (the place, for example, of a memorial, a portrait, or an epitaph), Norman has *become* his mother.

Figure 3.2 In *Psycho* (Hitchcock, 1960), Norman transformation into his aggressive mother manifests as a contradictory, disjointed, allegorical moment of confusion between past and present, fantasy and reality, self and other.

The trauma of a relationship of subjugation and aggression, coupled with an unresolved loss, causes "the shadow of the object" (S. Freud, 1917/1945) to fall over Norman's Ego and prevents him from separating emotionally from his mother or establishing a symbolic distance from her. The binarization that allows us to distinguish self from others (the mother from the son, in this case) has been dismantled by trauma; now, the two are one. This confuses us: are we facing Norman or his mother? Who is carrying the knife, who is the murderer, who is the victim in this film?

The lightbulb swings from the ceiling, casting a play of lights and shadows that move across Anthony Perkins' face (the actor who plays 'Norman'), who cannot quite be defined as the murderous old woman or the unremarkable manager of the semi-abandoned motel. The perceptual jumble, in shifting chiaroscuro, both discomforts and fascinates us; our gaze is trapped in the scene, striving to (re)process it.

Good horror narratives often move along a path that is more of a spiral than a forward line. In horror fiction, we would say, the irrational is more real than reality itself. The secondary process is subjected to the primary process. One of the fundamental manifestations of the latter is our dream life. Indeed, we believe that the horror narrative operates on a syntax equivalent to that of dreams: with lapses, ramifications, irrational fusions, an abolition of the laws of logic in favor of emotional and unconscious expression. And this makes sense from a perspective centered on the conflict we are often told about: the coexistence of emotions and ideas that cannot reconcile or be resolved into a cohesive narrative.

Repetition and its masks (I): Suffering from reminiscences

The birth of psychoanalysis occurred precisely in the wake of a discovery about the re-emergence of trauma. Freud (based on the work of predecessors such as Jean-Martin Charcot, Pierre Janet, and Joseph Breuer) deciphered the hitherto unexplained symptoms of patients suffering from hysteria. Hysteria was characterized by a complex picture of physical distress with no known medical cause. Hysterical blindness or paralysis, convulsions, anesthesia of unknown origin, or such bizarre symptoms as the inability to swallow water or the urgent need to urinate, among others, were, at that time, a catalogue of ailments that astonished the scientific community.

Through a combination of hypnosis and free association, Freud gradually discovered that underlying these strange symptoms was the memory of one or more traumas, often of a sexual nature. As children, unable to understand what was happening or to defend themselves, these patients had been victims of sexual abuse at the hands of an adult. The sexual content of these episodes, as it clashed head-on with the moral codes of the time (which weighed particularly heavily on women), had to be dissociated from the other contents of the self so that the victims could retain a socially acceptable identity.

As we have developed above, dissociation lays the basis for an anomalous transcription of experience. It remains outside the normal associative circuit that makes up the self-experience, and that would normally "soften" the impact of negative experiences. On the contrary, an effect similar to embalming is produced: the traumatic experience is stored in a state very similar to the original one, preserving its original intensity. And this is what Breuer and Freud attested to in their *Studies on Hysteria*: "[…] those memories which have become the causes of hysterical phenomena have persisted with almost undiminished clarity and the whole of their affective coloring" (1895, p. 10). The traumatic memory of these women survived as a foreign body, independent of the rest of mental life.

Freud continues at this point with an argument that will be central to psychoanalysis, and which has also been retained as commonplace in popular psychology: that which has not been processed tends to return. From the basement in which they hide, memories and traumatic emotions struggle to come to the surface. And it is here that the illness appears. The dissociated memory, in its effort to manifest itself, reappears hidden behind the mask of the symptom.

The conclusion reached by these authors points to an aspect of our mental life that is also central to the horror narrative: memory. According to them, the hysterical patient "suffers from reminiscences" (1895). What provokes the symptomatology of these patients is a painful memory, stored in an anomalous way, which manages to overcome the barriers of repression.

This is illustrated in two films that are decades apart but share a common metaphorical project: *Repulsion* (Polanski, 1965) and *Gerald's Game* (Flanagan, 2017).

Repulsion offers an interesting illustration of post-traumatic re-emergence. Despite her best efforts, Carol has been unable to prevent her sister from leaving for the weekend with her boyfriend, leaving her alone. A victim of childhood sexual abuse, and isolated for several days in their flat and in the big city of London, Carol will experience a descent into the hells of her traumatized mind. Polanski employs different metaphors to represent Carol's estrangement from herself and her progressive imbalance: a distorted reflection of her face on the teapot; the close-up of one of her eyes, open and paralyzed; the play of shadows and chiaroscuro that breaks the atmosphere of her house into patches of contradictory light; an erratic jazz soundtrack; the clutter of furniture, clothes and food; objects that progressively invade the space of the house (which, again, functions as a metaphor for the character's tormented mind). The film contains two particularly apt symbols in relation to the question of re-emergence. On the one hand, the wooden pieces with which Carol tries to board up her flat: a clear expression of the desire of her traumatized mind to erect a barrier to keep out her demons of the past. On the other hand, the crack, an image that presents itself to the protagonist in several scenes and that, as the story progresses, ends up becoming a persecutory motif. Towards the end of the film, Carol watches in terror as huge cracks open up in the walls, from which hands emerge, trying to touch and possess her. This is a metaphor for the re-emergence of the traumatic memory which, under the principles of the primary process, retains its original terrifying force.

Gerald's Game is a film based on a novel by Stephen King that, since its publication in 1992, had been considered impossible to film. Jessie and her husband Gerald retreat to an isolated country house, where, with the help of several doses of Viagra and unworn lingerie, they intend to rekindle their sex life and save their marriage. Gerald handcuffs Jessie to the bed and pressures her to indulge in a fantasy in which he plays the role of a rapist and she must pretend to be a victim, screaming helplessly for help. Uncomfortable, Jessie resists, at which point Gerald dies of a heart attack induced by the drug.

A nightmare begins for the bound protagonist, far from civilization, unable to call for help. As Jessie becomes dehydrated and panic sets in, a series of hallucinations plague her. In one, a strange, undefined figure appears to enter the house. A memory is triggered of when Jessie was twelve-years-old and her father sexually abused her. The past trauma is symbolically reproduced in her marriage to an impotent and aggressive man (Gerald) and imposes itself on her consciousness now that, under the effect of fear and weakness, repression has lost its effectiveness. The dark figure that raids her house brings with it the memory of the trauma that has been hidden for years; but, we discover, it also represents Jessie's chance to overcome her trauma.

Traumatic re-emergence can take on other masks. Some victims (the war veteran comes to mind) re-experience aspects of their trauma in a literal, very concrete and vivid version of what happened. Their memories have a strong sensory character (including images, sounds, smells, and bodily sensations associated with the traumatic event). They tend to burst abruptly into consciousness, often triggered by stimuli that, although objectively harmless, function as post-traumatic reminders: a friend suddenly approaching from behind, an intense and sudden sound on the road, the smell of burning, etc. In the face of these reminders, some people may experience intense emotional dysregulation and behavioral disturbances. Faced with his wife's initiation of a sexual game, the man who was sexually assaulted goes into a state of uncontrolled rage and threatens to kill her "if she does that again." The woman who was assaulted at night on her return home is, years later, overcome by non-specific anxiety attacks that paralyze her when she has to leave her home.

The bodies and minds of these people relive aspects of the trauma, often without reference to specific content that would allow a bridge to be established between the two experiences. These are actions triggered spontaneously and with an almost absolute capacity to dominate the victim's functioning.

Anne Erreich interprets this as the result of "imprinting:" trauma "imprints" the brain with a hypersensitivity to external cues, and a tendency to confirm a traumatic theory about the world. Some stimuli and situations are captured with particular acuity and interpreted as an anticipation (or a repetition) of the damage. She states that "traumatic events act as robust primes; they render individuals hyperalert for evocative elements of those events" (Erreich, 2017, p. 206).

Erreich relates the case of a female psychotherapist who had been sexually abused as a child. As an adult, this traumatic memory was encapsulated and did not seem to hinder her ability to lead a normal life. However, this woman entered into a relationship that led her to move in with her partner. Shortly after moving in with him, he psychologically abused her and threw her out of the house. In this way, she felt, once again, deceived and abused by a man who held a position of power over her. A traumatic content, strongly reactivated by this event, caused the woman to begin to experience severe anxiety reactions. On the clinical record sheets she had to fill in at the hospital where she worked, she often made the mistake of writing "the rapist" on the line where "therapist" should have been written. The current perception of having been abused triggered a rigid equation, an absence of the playful, dynamic metaphors that Modell describes as a centerpiece of emotional health. The current experience (with the partner) was merged with the past experience (with the father), blurring the boundary between past and present, and weakening the woman's ability to make rational discriminations between the two scenes (Erreich, 2017).

For subjects suffering from these conditions, the world becomes a threatening catalogue of situations, objects, people, and scenes that could reignite traumatic memories.

Repetition and its masks (II): Acting out the wound

Like children, traumatized adults are driven to reenact their painful experiences in more or less literal or camouflaged versions of the trauma. Years after the traumatic event, and without perceiving a connection between it and the present moment, the person is drawn into scenes or situations that bear an ominous resemblance to the original harm. Adults who were victims of childhood sexual abuse, for example, are more likely than others to find themselves in situations of sexual exploitation or in romantic relationships where they are again instrumentalized or subjugated by a partner (see Lalor and McElvaney, 2010). Re-victimization is also observable in some victims of domestic abuse, rejection, and marginalization, or other forms of interpersonal victimization. We find in all of them a tragic vulnerability to stumble over the same stone.

The psychodynamics of post-traumatic reenactment most likely involve a set of non-conscious fantasies and representations of the individual as 'condemned' to pain, perpetually exposed to danger, or in need of defending against it through defensive acts that, ironically, lead to new forms of harm (often experienced under the sign of the uncanny: an impression that this 'new' pain has something familiar and known) (Wachtel, 2014). This traumatic recursion, which relies on the subject's defensive attempts, is very reminiscent of the way (also ironic and distressing for the viewer) that characters in horror fiction, in their efforts to deny the existence of the monster, flee forward or rationalize the danger and its nature, thereby giving more strength to the threat and making themselves more vulnerable. Many of the traumatic experiences that take place early and chronically (often, within primary attachment relationships) may be stored at an unconscious level, in the form of "implicit relational knowledge" (Lyons-Ruth et al., 1998), as "forms of vitality" (Stern, 2010), or as a record of images, sounds, or affects stored in the right brain and dissociated from the circuitry of symbolization operating in the left brain (Hill, 2015). This forms a collection of unconscious schemas and fantasies that Monk refers to in terms of a "curse position" (2023). This trauma-derived unconscious complex is so named in Monk's work because it involves a representation of the self as devoid of agency and subject to the uncanny forces of unrepresented pain; a self that has had to submit to others in order to maintain attachments; or a self that is experienced as essentially inadequate or unworthy of the love of others. When people try to take these implicit representations into the territory of symbolization, they often construct narratives of the self based on an idea of fatality (a "secondary curse position" [Monk, 2023]): *I am a strange person and I have very bad luck; Nothing goes well for me; Why do these things always happen to me?;* etc. These stories that victims tell about themselves (what Freud thought of in terms of a "fate neurosis" [S. Freud, 1920/1961]) are often the narrative correlate of post-traumatic reenactments whereby, time after time (sometimes literally, sometimes through variations in form), people expose themselves (or others) to a repetition of traumatic harm, self-sabotage, or various forms of self-destructiveness.

Beverly, one of the main characters in *It* (Muschietti, 2017) is a young girl living in the poor area of Derry, with a father who sexually and physically abuses her. In her childhood confrontation with Pennywise (the clown-like evil entity who stalks the protagonists), he tortures her with images of her father's abuse and violence (a post-traumatic re-experiencing very similar to what PTSD patients suffer). Years later, Beverly is an attractive and successful adult who has no memory of the violence she suffered as a child. However, she is married to an abusive man. Her trauma is not replayed in the form of flashbacks or dreams, but in a behavioral format: a relationship in which Beverly is once again a victim. Moreover, in one of the novel's climactic moments, an episode occurs that is shocking and problematic for the reader – so problematic, in fact, that it was ostensibly toned down in the film version: as a coming-of-age ritual, before she crosses a certain threshold, the girl proposes that all the boys have sex with her. Although King has since explained that he was not interested in the sexual aspect of the situation, but in its symbolism, it is hard not to think of Beverly's circumstances and how her father's abuse may have conditioned her understanding of sex.

Re-victimization is often the paradoxical result of the traumatized person's attempts to avoid further harm. Richard Kluft describes the case of a woman who, as a child, was exposed to her father's outbursts of uncontrolled rage, which often culminated in brutal physical punishment (2017). With time and age, she discovered that an attitude of coyness and surrender was helpful in preventing these attacks, which led to sexual abuse at the hands of her father a few years later. Now an adult, she recounts in therapy how she has gone through several relationships in which she indulges in rarely consensual sexual encounters based on submission. Whenever a man is angry with her, the woman tends to adopt sexual attitudes (for example, she unbuttons her blouse) without realizing what she is doing, experiencing the scene "from the outside." As we explained, this dynamic of post-traumatic re-enactment is closely linked to the victim's efforts to protect herself.

Her strategies to appease the aggressor (in the form of sexualized behavior) have a paradoxical effect: they increase her vulnerability to being subjected once again. A vicious circle of traumatic repetition crystallizes.

Exposing oneself to unnecessary dangers, sabotaging opportunities for achievement or enjoyment, and attacking one's self-esteem and well-being can be other ways of unconsciously acting out aspects of a traumatic experience that has left the person with essential feelings of shame, moral degradation, or guilt.

We find an exploration of these aspects in *Annihilation* (Garland, 2018), based on the novel of the same name by Jeff Vandermeer. The film starts – once again – with a blocked grief: a year after her husband Kane disappeared on a military mission, Lena, a university biology professor, still has not moved on. She works mechanically, refuses social invitations, and spends her weekends at home, waiting for her husband to return. At the center of this blocked grief is a guilt of traumatic proportions: Kane volunteered for that mysterious (and, we will soon learn, suicidal) mission when he found out that Lena was being unfaithful with a coworker. Lena is trapped in a loop of grief and guilt from which she finds it impossible to escape until, suddenly, Kane shows up back at the house. Lena quickly discovers that the man in front of her is a strange variation of her husband: an alien replica? The real Kane, but alienated? Determined to unravel the mystery and redeem herself, Lena sets out on a foray into Zone X, the place where Kane disappeared: a space in the south of the United States that appears to have been colonized by some kind of extraterrestrial entity fallen from the sky.

The scientists with whom Lena takes on this mission are women ravaged by loss, alcoholism, or self-destructiveness ("damaged goods," says one of them) and Zone X reveals itself as a catalyst for these women's traumatic demons. From her first night in the Zone, reminders of her trauma are forced upon Lena: she dreams of her infidelity, Kane's departure, their farewell. Post-traumatic flashbacks become more frequent as they go deeper into the Zone. Radio or GPS signals are unable to pass through the iridescent dome that delimits the Zone and are refracted back into it, increasing the impression of solipsism and of being inside a mental or symbolic space. Refraction is, in fact, the essential logic that dominates everything in the region: plants take on human form or animals reproduce sounds identical to the voices of the protagonists. Zone X is a mirroring space, and Lena's journey is an inner journey: a path of encounter with herself.

In a recording found inside the lighthouse where the alien matter originally fell, Lena discovers that the Zone, through its refractory properties, has created a replica of her husband. Lena descends to the underground levels of the lighthouse where she is faced with a choice: letting herself be annihilated by the alien intelligence or keeping her life and returning to the world and the double of Kane, the empty and anomalous version of her dead husband that also represents a second chance to atone for her faults and regain love.

Finally, traumatic re-enactments can take the form of a repetition in which the victim–offender role distribution is reversed, and the traumatized subject is now the perpetrator of harms very similar to those they received. For some traumatized adults, inflicting injury on others may be a desperate way of regaining some sense of power in the face of the devastating suffering of their own traumas, or of making some sense of their suffering by seeing it reflected in others (A. Freud, 1936). Research confirms that a significant proportion of abusive parents themselves come from violent backgrounds, in which they were victims (Thornberry & Henry, 2013). The psyche of these people seems to be tied to a scene that it strives to repeat, over and over again, albeit by reversing the distribution of power and damage.

Perhaps *In a Glass Cage* (Villaronga, 1986) contains the starkest and most disturbing representation of this reversal. After the Second World War, Klaus, a German doctor responsible for terrible experiments and torture during the Holocaust, takes refuge in Franco's Spain. Klaus is now a sick man who depends on an iron lung (a large mechanical pod) to breathe. The film shows him in a state of maximum vulnerability, lying passive and immobile inside the iron lung that keeps him alive, cared for by his wife and daughter.

One day, Angelo, a young man who claims to be a nurse and is hired by Klaus's wife to take care of his basic needs, shows up at the house. For years, Angelo was the victim of atrocious sexual torture inflicted by the young Klaus. Today, the roles are reversed, and Klaus finds himself, stripped of all power, in the hands of his former victim. Soon, we witness a sequence of different tortures and humiliations administered by Angelo on the helpless body of his torturer. In one scene, Angelo disconnects the respirator, leaving Klaus gasping like a fish out of water, on the verge of asphyxiation. In another, Angelo masturbates on top of the German's motionless face.

However, the most disturbing aspects of this settling of scores come in the form of Angelo emulating the tortures he received from Klaus on children he himself abducts in the vicinity of the house. Angelo shows Klaus the end product of the sexual abuse he was subjected to: he is now a monster like his torturer. Angelo befriends a young boy, whom he takes to Klaus' room, where he abuses and murders him by injecting poison into his heart, in front of a terrified Klaus who cannot stop watching. A flashback shows Klaus forcing young Angelo to perform fellatio on him; a scene from the present shows Angelo forcing another boy to sing sweetly to Klaus seconds before Angelo slits his throat.[2] At the end of the story, the mental disorder caused by the trauma materializes in a dismantled house, with the furniture thrown out, and burning at its center. In the last scene, Klaus is dead, and we see Angelo entering the iron lung, culminating his identification with the aggressor, making his transformation into his torturer definitive.

A Gothic nightmare: The transmission of trauma between generations

One of the most fascinating and disturbing forms of post-traumatic repetition is that which transcends the individual sphere and takes place from one generation to the next. We are struck by the capacity of trauma to re-emerge again and again in the individual's life in the formats we have described above (dreams, unconscious repetition of the same misfortunes, intrusive thoughts and emotions).

But it is even more shocking that the trauma of one generation re-emerges in the life of the next generation, that the wounds of the parents are reproduced in the child.

Parents who carry histories of intense pain or unresolved loss are potentially vulnerable to raising their children in ways analogous to how they themselves were harmed. A child whose mother has a history of child maltreatment is 50% more likely to experience maltreatment compared to a child whose mother had a protected childhood. More than half of children aged 1–5 years whose mothers experienced maltreatment have been victimized themselves. The likelihood of children experiencing maltreatment at the hands of their mothers increases by 300% when their mothers experienced a combination of trauma (abuse and neglect) in the family (J.D. Bartlett et al., 2017).

The terrifying nature of this phenomenon captured the attention of Selma Fraiberg, one of the first clinicians concerned with uncovering the invisible logics of the intergenerational transmission of trauma. She titled her pioneering work using a metaphor central to the horror narrative, "Ghosts in the nursery" (Fraiberg, Adelson, & Shapiro, 1975):

> In every nursery there are ghosts. They are visitors from the unremembered past of the parents; the uninvited guests at the christening.
>
> (1975, p. 387)

These words suggest that no family is immune to this unconscious remembrance: welcoming the new baby means, irrevocably, reconnecting with one's own childhood (Slade & Cohen, 1996). In most cases, Fraiberg says, the child and its overwhelming fragility mobilize parental care:

> Under all favorable circumstances the unfriendly and unbidden spirits are banished from the nursery and return to their subterranean dwelling place. The baby makes his own imperative claim upon parental love and, in strict analogy with the fairy tales, the bonds of love protect the child and his parents against the intruders, the malevolent ghosts.
>
> (1975, p. 387)

However, there are families where the traces of the parental past are so dark that the child functions as a catalyst for the ghosts that, for years, rested in the basement of the mind:

> The intruders from the past have taken up residence in the nursery, claiming tradition and rights of ownership. They have been present at the christening for two or more generations. While no one has issued an invitation, the ghosts take up residence and conduct the rehearsal of the family tragedy from a tattered script.
>
> (1975, p. 388)

The work of Fraiberg and her colleagues delves into a clinical analysis of the mechanisms of trauma transmission in those families whose generations seem haunted by the legacy of violence, sexual abuse, or neglect. According to the authors, the child functions as a powerful post-traumatic reminder for these damaged parents. Their dependency and fragility push parents to connect with the moments in their history when they themselves were dependent and fragile, and with the responses they received from the environment at that time. Some gestures or behaviors of the child drag the parent back to a past scene. These parents' brains are flooded with old emotions, very difficult to modulate, and which hijack the system.

These parents are faced with difficult questions: What to do in the face of such a flood of anxiety that one thought one had overcome? How to regain one's balance, one's sense of control? In short, how to escape from the (always unwelcome) feeling of being a helpless child again? For some of these parents, a desperate solution to this unbearable pain is to *identify with the aggressor*. By adopting the same attitudes and emulating the responses of their own aggressor parents, traumatized adults can avoid feeling helpless in the face of trauma and regain a sense of power in the face of what is happening, an impression of control. Hurting others is a way of not feeling hurt again. Controlling, demanding, and becoming critical is a way of not feeling exposed to the humiliation and criticism of the past. Neglecting the child puts the rejected parent in a place of power: now they are the one who turns her back, rather than the one who suffers abandonment.

The same drama is reproduced with equivalent roles (the aggressor and the victim, someone who humiliates and someone who is humiliated) only that, in this iteration of the story, the distribution of these roles is reversed. Traumatic ghosts infiltrate the experience of both participants. For the parent, the child has been replaced by the image of a previous aggressor or an unbearable scene from the past; for the child, the parent (usually a caregiver) is replaced by a dangerous adult whom it is suddenly impossible to recognize (perhaps those fairy tales in which a warm maternal figure disguises a witch or a ravenous wolf were meant to represent the confusion and terror of the child who sees their primary caregivers transformed into monsters).

The processes that sustain the transmission of trauma do not end here: they also occur at a deep, structural level of our biological functioning. Beyond the attitudes and parenting practices of damaged parents, science suggests that there is also a genetic transmission of emotional wounds. Trauma produces changes in the genetic expression of victims, and these changes can be inherited by the children and grandchildren of the traumatized person.

Data found in children and grandchildren of Holocaust survivors are of particular relevance. These subjects, in the absence of direct exposure to trauma, show nervous system alterations that would be typical of a subject with post-traumatic stress disorder (Yehuda & Lerner, 2018). Yehuda suggests that these second and third generation Holocaust descendants:

> [...] live their lives as if somebody is gunning for them, as if somebody is hunting them down, as if somebody wants to hurt them, even though they've never actually had that experience consciously, but it's almost as if they're feeling hunted anyway, or feeling vulnerable anyway.
>
> (Yehuda, 2023)

A substantial body of laboratory data from rodents points in a direction very similar to the results described above. Compared to well-nourished rat offspring whose parents have lived in a relatively safe environment, rat offspring whose parents have been administered various stressors are born with a nervous system that is particularly sensitive to stress, with greater difficulties in fear regulation, and with a range of physiological markers (for example, a poorer immune response) that are common in traumatized subjects. As mentioned above, these alterations, in the absence of a direct impact of the trauma on the offspring, respond to the genetic alteration that the original trauma produced in the victims, and which would have been transferred intergenerationally (Meany & Szyf, 2005).

We speak of an epigenetic effect when any stressor (lack of food, violence, loss, etc.) can cause changes in gene expression (what we call the 'phenotype') without altering the underlying genetic code (what we call the 'genotype'). Epigenetics brings us face to face with an astonishing fact: DNA – that part of our biological constitution that we thought was unchanging and fixed, subject only to change through mutation – is sensitive to the effects of the environment. This is not without logic: it makes sense that the traumatic learning of one generation becomes heritable, so that the next generation is born a little more prepared – or at least genetically 'warned' – for a hostile environment, even if it has not had a direct encounter with that hostility. Traumatic 'wisdom' tends to pass from parents to children, and from children to grandchildren, through a hereditary process that would complement the mechanisms explained above (the post-traumatic re-experiencing of parents, and their need to protect themselves through acts that may traumatize their own children).

Paradoxes of traumatic parenthood in three horror films

Annie, the already mentioned protagonist of *Hereditary* (Aster, 2018), embodies one of the fundamental aspects of the transmission of trauma from parents to children. At the beginning of the film, Annie defines herself as a survivor of a dynasty that has been plagued by madness, violence, and secrecy. She herself knows that, with her mother's recent death, the aggressive undercurrents of her emotional and family life are stirring again, threatening to provoke an undertow whose victims would be her own children. She has experienced firsthand the effects that maternal rage and manipulation can have, and she has fought for years against the eruption of these feelings by creating miniature models in which she represents and contains her experiences. Recreated in miniature, life does not seem as threatening, and it does not overflow and become the nightmare Annie senses beneath every ordinary moment.

Annie, in short, is a mother in conflict. On the one hand there are the influences inherited from her mother, that destructiveness that could befall her children if left unchecked (the 'ghosts' Fraiberg spoke of). On the other hand, there are her efforts to keep her sanity and maintain a protective distance from Peter (her secretive teenager) and Charlie (her strange daughter who clicks her tongue and draws goggle-eyed faces). And this is most likely a central feature of the experience of traumatized parents: the struggle not to repeat the harms of which they were victims and the attempt to keep the voice of the parents themselves at bay. Although the victims in *Hereditary* are the younger members of the family, the real (tragic) heroine of the film is Annie.

Two other films allegorize the intergenerational repetition of the traumatic in highly suggestive ways. In *Dark Water* (Nakata, 2002), Yoshimi, a young mother going through a divorce, struggles to keep custody of her daughter Ikuko, get a job, and find a new flat for the two of them to live in. Yoshimi's most crucial struggle, however, is to spare her daughter the emotional neglect she herself suffered as a child.

The film opens with a clear allusion to this conflict, the backbone of the story. Through a rain-soaked window, we see Yoshimi's sad face, waiting for her appointment with a lawyer. The next shot is of another rain-covered window and, on the other side, the face of Ikuko, who is also waiting alone at nursery for her mother to come and pick her up. Later on the film offers us images of Yoshimi, as a child, waiting in vain to be picked up by her own parents. These scenes are like beads on a rosary, where loneliness and abandonment repeat for both characters.

Overwhelmed by the complex demands of her situation, Yoshimi keeps making the mistake she has set out to avoid: she forgets her daughter, she is late to pick her up, or her own emotional overflow prevents her from being available. And the story presents Yoshimi as a woman who is victimized (mainly by her ex-husband) and fragile, suggesting that her struggle to keep custody of Ikuko is not only a desire to care for her, but also a desire to avoid being alone again. Our protagonist is therefore in a fragile emotional equilibrium, trying to keep the effects of her past trauma at bay and to prevent its repetition on her daughter.

The traumatic then finds its definitive channel of expression (and repetition) when mother and daughter move into a new flat in a grey, gridded block of flats. Here, a series of strange events begins to take place. A leak appears in the bedroom ceiling. As the days go by, the leak grows until water penetrates the house in several areas and the protective boundaries that Yoshimi had tried to build around her and her daughter are revealed to be a fragile shell. Then a mysterious little girl appears in the upstairs hallway and peeks through the door of the flat directly above theirs: it is from there, where the pale girl lives, that the water from the leak seeps in. Finally, there is the insidious reappearance of a red backpack that they had supposedly thrown away at least twice. Where does it come from? How does the strange object make its way back into their lives? Above all, what does it represent?

Yoshimi asks the building manager to show him the flat upstairs, which he finds empty and dry (but, then, where does the huge amount of water dripping into their flat come from?) Later, she discovers that the girl she has seen walking around the building disappeared a year ago. This girl, the owner of the reappearing red backpack, had also been abandoned by her parents, and on one of her solitary, unsupervised walks fell into the water tank on the roof of the building, where she died.

The wound of abandonment, which binds these three characters together, enters horror territory when the ghost girl threatens to murder (by drowning) Ikuko unless Yoshimi agrees to an uncanny deal: if Yoshimi stays with her and cares for her like a mother, the ghost girl will allow Ikuko to live. Yoshimi agrees and sacrifices herself, in a powerful scene in which Ikuko watches as her mother, from inside the lift, shouts, "Stay away!" and, before the doors close, turns to the ghost girl and says, "I am your mother now." A gigantic wave of water then rushes towards little Ikuko, who has been left alone in the same way that her own mother and her ghostly neighbor had been. Her mother, in a desperate attempt to protect her daughter, has inadvertently identified herself with the aggressor; now it is she who inflicts abandonment equivalent to that which she herself suffered.

According to Arnold, this ending contains a painful ambiguity: "The mother resolves her own feelings of abandonment by acting as mother figure to the little ghost girl but also steps back from her own daughter […]" (2016, p. 133). The ambiguity here comes from the fact that, in this act of perverse self-sacrifice, Yoshimi, by making Ikuko safe from danger, leaves her alone. And, more disturbingly, Yoshimi obtains a certain compensation for her own abandonment, by caring for a girl who is clearly more dependent (and voracious) than her own daughter.

Color Out of Space (Stanley, 2019) is a cosmic horror film that exploits a Lovecraft story (while ostensibly departing from it) to also explore the distorting effect of trauma on parent-child relationships. In its opening scene, the film shows us Lavinia, the daughter of the Gardner family, performing a wicca ritual designed to prevent the breakdown of her family. Lavinia, a perceptive and openly concerned teenager, is the only character who does not use denial to survive the difficulties her family are experiencing. She recognizes the latent tensions that have been affecting her family since her mother had to undergo a mastectomy and they moved away from the city to settle on a farm that had belonged to her paternal grandfather. Midway through the film, in fact, Lavinia's ritualistic efforts to keep the evil that threatens her family at bay increase in intensity: we see her carving the word "solve" into her skin with a knife, when it is already clear that the Gardners are being dragged towards disaster.

In a clear flight forward, Nathan and Theresa, the parents, pretend that the new life they are building in the countryside is idyllic: they joke artificially at the dinner table, unjustifiably uncork bottles of wine reserved for celebrations, and force themselves to feel good, to be happy. These efforts fail to conceal the fact that both parents are absorbed in their own affairs and are always one step away from becoming irritated and furious with their children. We soon discover that not only does the traumatic shadow of Theresa's cancer loom over them, but also that Nathan was the victim of abuse at the hands of his own father, on the farm where they have begun their new life. Away from their children's gaze, both adults recognize that they may be becoming a version of their own parents, something they had always promised themselves to avoid.

That night, a meteorite falls in the garden of the farmhouse, fulfilling the function that we have been attributing to the monstrous throughout this essay: to metaphorize the hidden, reemergent forces of trauma. After the meteorite falls, a strange, alien color emanates from the well on the farm. New species of plants and fruits begin to grow in the garden, also endowed with strange colors and proportions. Nathan, whose mental breakdown is becoming increasingly apparent, oscillates between excitement and terror as he witnesses the metamorphoses taking place in his home. Theresa absent-mindedly cuts her finger while preparing dinner, and Nathan has to take her to the emergency room. During the period when the children are separated from their parents, all electronic devices stop working, preventing them from contacting them, while the livestock on the farm begin to behave abnormally. Family ties are being invaded, distorted by the color emanating from the meteorite. The structure crumbles.

Eventually Nathan descends into a spiral of alcoholism and begins to display the abusive, violent behavior that we know his father had used against him. Identification with the aggressor comes into play as we see Nathan become his own father.

Stephen King writes that horror stories are dedicated to touching on the "phobic pressure points" specific to each culture and each historical moment, those "fears which exist across a wide spectrum of people" (1981, p. 63). (One of his examples is that of American horror films which, during the Cold War, exhibited a cohort of monsters that were the product of nuclear research.) Phobic pressure points contain the nightmare that beats behind the harmonious and civilized face of culture.

Applying King's argument, films such as *Hereditary*, *Dark Water* and *Color Out of Space* explore phobic concerns that underlie our idealization of the family and parent–child relationships. Ideals of dedication, care, sacrifice, and generosity that define parental (mostly, maternal) imagery, and the spirit of cohesion and brightness that we associate with the family, crack at those points where pain, stress, or anger turn the parental dream into a nightmare.

Notes

1 The amygdala is a finicky organ: defensive responses can be triggered by objectively harmless stimuli that have nevertheless been interpreted as threatening. Thus, if we are walking in the forest and our foot lands on a branch that might look like a snake, our amygdala makes a conservative interpretation (*if it looks like a snake, it is a snake*) and quickly triggers an automatic defence response. This tendency of the amygdala to overestimate danger is closely linked to our survival.

2 The scenes we describe are so disturbing that, at the end of the film, the producers chose to introduce a message assuring that no children were abused during the making of the film.

Chapter 4

The hero's darkest journey

Trauma storytelling in modern horror film

This chapter approaches the subject matter from a slightly different angle. It investigates the narrative mechanisms of trauma storytelling in modern horror cinema, emphasizing how these films metaphorically represent the processes of trauma re-emergence and coping. It posits that horror narratives often follow a pattern: protagonists must transition from denial and rationalization to acceptance of supernatural phenomena, ultimately confronting their fears in acts of extreme courage and risk. This narrative journey mirrors the psychological stages of trauma recovery.

The chapter identifies two primary storytelling models in horror films. The first involves protagonists encountering unexpected traumatic events without prior psychological baggage, as seen in *Alien* (R. Scott, 1979) or *The Texas Chainsaw Massacre* (Hooper, 1974). The second model, more central to this analysis, involves traumatic re-emergence plots where unresolved psychic traumas manifest through supernatural threats, as exemplified by *The Babadook* (Kent, 2014) and *His House* (Weekes, 2020).

The chapter further explores the dissolution of conventional authority and the role of alternative figures, such as mediums or experts in the occult, who guide protagonists through their supernatural ordeals. This is likened to shamanic rituals where new symbolic systems help articulate unformulated traumatic experiences.

Key narrative stages are identified: sightings of uncanny phenomena, resistance through rational denial, acceptance of the supernatural, and the climactic trance where protagonists confront their fears. The need to name and understand the monstrous threat is crucial, providing a framework to process trauma. The chapter concludes that horror films, through their unique narrative structures, offer profound insights into the psychological processes of trauma recovery, highlighting the transformative power of confronting and integrating traumatic experiences.

As mentioned above, our premise is that much contemporary horror fiction can be interpreted as a metaphorical representation of processes of re-emergence and coping with trauma. In the following pages, we will examine in greater detail how this process unfolds narratively; that is, we will explore what we believe to be a narrative pattern present in a good number of modern horror films, and within which many of the metaphors of traumatic phenomenology described in the previous sections are produced. We can anticipate that the path to any outcome of assimilation or overcoming will necessarily pass through several milestones: first,

DOI: 10.4324/9781003468981-5

it is imperative that the protagonist desists from attempts at escape through denial or rationalization (for example, "There must be a scientific explanation for what is happening in this house"), and accepts the nature – often supernatural, and always alien to rational logic – of the phenomenon that haunts them. This acceptance will lead them to seek help beyond conventional authorities (police, scientists), which have already proved incapable of understanding, let alone solving their problem. Here the figure of the 'medium' or the expert in the occult fulfils a function comparable to that of the sorcerer in shamanic rituals, providing a new system of symbols, a language through which the unformulated and informulable states of trauma can be expressed in another way (Lévi-Strauss, 1987, p. 221). Finally, a fundamental condition of this trance's success, after the renunciation of flight and the acquisition of useful new knowledge by the protagonist, is that the protagonist voluntarily approaches the object of their fear. Even if the monster never gives in and pursues its relentless siege to the end, we invariably observe that there comes a point in the narrative where the protagonist comes to terms with the inescapable reality of the situation and exposes himself to the creature in an act of extreme courage and risk. We could even say that the simple gesture of leaving shelter and looking the monster in the face, even though it may seem like a sacrificial surrender, is already a victory in that it demonstrates the overcoming of fear.

Two models of storytelling

It is worth starting by clarifying that, according to our analysis, the trauma motif is typically presented in two ways in horror narrative structures. In the first model, (a good example of which would be the film *Alien* [R. Scott, 1979]), what is narrated is the protagonist's encounter with a totally unexpected and potentially violent event, which shatters their basic assumptions and is therefore experienced as traumatic. In these fictions, the protagonist is in a sense a *tabula rasa*, they do not carry a troubled past or a psychological complex that can be clearly identified with the present terrifying event. In other words, the monster has no 'personal vendetta' against them, their experiences are not the symptom of dissociated traumatic contents or unconscious conflicts. So it is with Ripley and the rest of the crew of the starship Nostromo, with the young protagonists of *The Texas Chainsaw Massacre* (Hooper, 1974), or with the protagonists of almost any zombie film.

The second type of story (a good example of which would be the film *The Babadook* [Kent, 2014]) could be called traumatic 're-emergence plots' – these are the ones that focus our attention in this essay; they narrate the protagonist's confrontation with a phenomenon or a creature that embodies, in a more or less obvious way, unresolved psychic trauma, and whose return has been brought about by a triggering event or by a change in the protagonist's life circumstances.

The death of the father in *The Babadook* or the loss of the supposed daughter in *His House* are revealed at the end of each story as unequivocal causes of the terrifying events that follow, and the defeat of the monster is consequently identified with the overcoming of trauma (Weekes, 2020).

It is important to remember that the monster does not embody trauma in a single way, but can function as a *condensation* of several disorders, in the style of a mythological chimera. In *The Babadook*, for example, the monster represents, in addition to the trauma of the loss of the husband, the mother's unacknowledged rejection of the son, the son's hatred of a mother who is ambivalent towards him, and the weight of social expectations and demands placed on a single mother with a troubled child.

Further, we could say that the monster does not exactly represent the tragic or traumatic event itself (the loss of the husband), which can no longer be changed, but rather the protagonist's *inability to* cope with this loss and its emotional consequences (something we have alluded to in previous pages in terms of a difficulty in processing painful events or an anomalous registration of them). The symptoms that horror fiction metaphorizes as monsters arise from this inability to assimilate.

On many occasions, what is narrated is the synchronization of the protagonist's present and personal conflict – not necessarily traumatic; it can be an anxiety, an intimate frustration or a depressive state – with someone else's traumatic history. This is what happens in stories where the protagonists move into houses or places where terrible events took place, as for example in *Sinister* (Derrickson, 2012). Ellison Oswald is a novelist whose career has been stalled for some time and decides to move with his family to a house where multiple murders took place in order to write a new successful novel. The discovery of a box of home movies in the attic, which Ellison begins to watch while locked in his office, connects the author's present obsession – to regain a sense of triumph and recognition – with the horrors of the past. By the time the creepy apparitions begin to occur and the protagonist decides it is best to leave the house, it is too late: the simple act of moving into the house and watching the videos has already led to the inclusion of his own family in the cursed chain.

It is common, moreover, for a single event to reactivate different traumatic contents in various main characters. For example, in *The Exorcist*, although the adversary is the same for everyone – the demon Pazuzu – the 'personal demons' it awakens in Regan (her entry into adolescence in the absence of her father and under the threat of her mother bringing in an 'imposter' father) are not the same as those that besiege her mother (a professionally successful actress with an unstable love life and an overwhelmed mother), nor those that assail Jesuit priest Damien Karras (immersed in a crisis of faith and plagued by guilt for not having properly cared for his deceased mother), nor those that confront Father Merrin (who, with a heart condition, knows he will not survive another encounter with his eternal adversary) (Friedkin, 1973). This would be, therefore, a new form of condensation of meanings, in this case originating from a chorus of characters.

A possible structure of horror

Looking for a synthesis of the works of John Clute and Noël Carroll, and focusing only on the model of stories with a traumatic basis, we can recognize a very common narrative structure, divided into four narrative movements, which we will call: 'sightings,' 'resistance,' 'acceptance,' and 'trance.'

Sightings

The writer John Clute uses the term "sightings" to refer to the first narrative movement in horror stories. According to his definition, the sighting is the first sign that something is about to take us away from the map of the normal world. Appealing to Freud's concept of *"unheimlich"* (S. Freud, 1919/1945), Clute describes the process of discovering that the protagonist's familiar surroundings are in fact a *trompe l'oeil*, an illusion concealing the unbearable truth, as uncanny. The sighting thus signifies the appearance of the first crack in normality: the fleeting manifestation of an anomalous event, the arrival of a strange personage, etc. There is still no way of knowing how deep the abyss underneath is, and the protagonist is far from recognizing the hidden 'familiarity' of the phenomenon, but they perceive that they have lost their footing in their basic assumptions. In psychological terms, one could conceptualize the sightings as non-specific symptoms of trauma. As we have seen, many patients with post-traumatic stress disorder (PTSD) suffer from physical problems without medical cause: headaches, abdominal pain, insomnia, or a general state of physiological over-arousal, for example. Many of these symptoms are closely related to their trauma (for example, abdominal pain in someone who has been raped or sexually abused), but patients find it impossible to make the connection. The phenomenology of Freudian *après-coup* may also involve a subjective experience reminiscent of the glimpses described by Clute. Confronted with a present situation (for example, an uncomfortable sexual interaction), the subject is forced to "revisit" previous experiences that bear some resemblance to the current experience, but which could not be processed (for example, childhood sexual abuse). In the light of current events, these previous unmetabolized episodes take on a gravity and an impression of taboo, injustice, or shame that was not present in the original experience. An *'a posteriori'* trauma is formed, from the present to the past. This act of resignification brings very negative consequences for the person, henceforth; however, during the current episode, the person's subjective experience is reduced to an unformulated distress (*I don't like this; this is wrong; something bad is going to happen*), an incipient unrest, the anticipation of something that cannot yet be fully formulated: a series of glimpses.

Due to the re-emergent nature of trauma, repetition or 'cyclicity' is a common pattern in these narrative structures: the horrific events of the present are a repetition, more or less exacerbated, of something that happened before. We have mentioned *It* as a paradigmatic example (the 'losers' club' reunites 27 years later to re-fight the creature they faced in their childhood) (Muschietti, 2017); in *The Thing*, the events that take place at an American research station are an almost identical repetition of what happened shortly before at a Norwegian research station (Carpenter, 1982); in many 'slashers,' it is common for the killer to return on special dates (*Halloween* [Carpenter, 1978], *Friday the 13th* [Cunningham, 1980],

My Bloody Valentine [Mihalka, 1981], etc); in *Midsommar*, everything takes place during the annual summer holiday celebration (Aster, 2019); the creature in *Jeepers Creepers* returns every twenty-three springs (Salva, 2001); in *The Shining* we know that Jack Torrance is not the first Overlook caretaker to lose his mind and murder his family... (Kubrick, 1980).

It is common for unease to progressively set in as the story progresses and for our restlessness to grow in sync with that of the protagonist. In *Hereditary*, the first minute of the film conveys sensations of strangeness, vigilance, and splitting through a visual game of houses within houses, to immediately afterwards immerse us in the gloomy and cold atmosphere of the grandmother's funeral (Aster, 2018).

Other films start directly with the traumatic scene or a glimpse of it. This is the case in *Smile* (Finn, 2022) (the mother's suicide), *The Babadook* (Kent, 2014) (the car accident in which the husband dies), *The Changeling* (Medak, 1980) (the wife and daughter are run over by a truck), *Don't Look Now* (Roeg, 1973) (the daughter dies in the lake) and *Midsommar* (Aster, 2019) (the sister's suicide and the murder of the parents).

In any case – in this, horror is no different from any other narrative genre – the story must always present a change in the circumstances surrounding the protagonist. Often this is a voluntary and desired change, for example, a move or a stay in a house that turns out to be haunted. And as has already been said, what is the haunted house if not a physical representation of the protagonist's 'haunted' mind? What are the basement, the attic, or the locked room if not spaces of the dissociated unconscious where unformulated emotions and traumatic memories are hidden? The examples are innumerable: *The Haunting* (Wise, 1963), *The Shining* (Kubrick, 1980), *His House* (Weekes, 2020), *Barbarian* (Cregger, 2022), *The Night House* (Bruckner, 2020).

Obviously, the house is only one of the possible scenarios. The key element is the transit towards an 'other' place, towards "heterotopia," to use Foucault's term (1967/2008). These are places normally isolated in space – a house in the suburbs, a ship in the middle of the sea, or a ship sailing through space would be paradigmatic examples – and also separated in time – here Foucault distinguishes between places where time stands still (an old colonial house, an abandoned village) and places subject to a festive or cyclical time (Halloween night, the festival in *Midsommar (Aster, 2019)* – in a manner reminiscent of Eliade's division between sacred and profane spaces and times (1964). In primitive societies, says Foucault, these privileged or sacred places were reserved for individuals in "biological crisis:" special enclosures for adolescents at the time of puberty, for women in their menstrual period or giving birth... (1967/2008). In our society, he concludes, heterotopias for individuals in biological crisis have practically disappeared. But we might think that fiction continues to invent and choose these 'other' places, clearly differentiated from the rest, to stage the psychological crises of the protagonists.

There is usually a physical boundary or barrier that the protagonist must cross to reach that special place. It can be a lake that has to be rowed across (*The Night House* [Bruckner, 2020], *The Birds* [Hitchcock, 1963]), a secret door in the basement (*Barbarian* [Cregger, 2022]), a border of a fantastic or technological nature (*The Cabin in the Woods* [Goddard, 2012], *Annihilation* [Garland, 2018]), etc.

The paradigmatic transit in all horror fiction, in any case, takes place at twilight. All the terrifying connotations of night – from which the horror genre generously draws – stem from an obvious biological basis: when the sun disappears over the horizon and darkness falls, we human beings become vulnerable creatures, exposed to what lies beyond our limited capacity for vision. As Quammen says: "Among the earliest forms of human self-awareness was the awareness of being meat" (2003, p. 20); and our natural environment was not populated by specters or witches, but by hungry and very real nocturnal predators. The luminous hours of the day, full of possibilities, are thus transformed into dark and dangerous hours, but also into hours of obligatory surrender to sleep. Under normal circumstances, our brain, organized in circadian rhythms, begins to produce melatonin when night falls to promote the onset of sleep. In this way, twilight is also associated with the transition from waking life to dream life, so to speak, and the dream world is the ultimate heterotopia: the place of the primary process, where different rules apply, where the boundary between the possible and the impossible is blurred in an emotional, non-rational logic, where time is suspended and the dead can talk with the living without any problem.

These transits do not always require a physical displacement. It is enough that there is an alteration of the environment in which the protagonist had managed, until now, to deal with their own ghosts in an acceptable way, ignoring them or veiling them behind a series of routines that allowed them to function relatively normally. The transition is in any case a mental one, and involves the disappearance of the protective barriers that had hitherto kept the protagonist's traumas or unresolved issues at bay. In *The Babadook*, for example, Amelia has managed to overcome the confrontation with her trauma (the death of her husband) through strategies such as isolation, abandoning work, or celebrating her son Samuel's birthday on a different date than his real birth date, instead making him share a party with his cousin (Kent, 2014). Only when her sister decides to put an end to this habit (the children detest each other) is Amelia forced to face the critical anniversary. At the same time, Samuel's behavior has become so violent that Amelia is forced to remove him from his school, and the confrontations between mother and son reach a level that is no longer bearable for either of them. It is then – after the threat of the impending birthday and quasi-expulsion from school – that Amelia finds *The Babadook* book on the shelves; what follows is the manifestation of Amelia's symptoms in the form of an invading monster.

We could conclude that traumatic re-emergence is almost always facilitated by some factor that disrupts the previous defensive equilibrium. It may be an increase in the intensity of contents that were dissociated/repressed (for example, contents associated with childhood sexual abuse may be 'dormant' until the person becomes sexually active as an adult, at which point they gain new strength). It may be a lowering of dissociative barriers (in states of sleep, fatigue, accumulated stress, illness, substance use, hypnosis, etc.). It could be an encounter with reminders (anniversaries of the traumatic event, a face, object or setting reminiscent of the trauma, testifying against the perpetrator when they are on trial, etc.). Or – and this is where the likelihood of traumatic re-experiencing increases dramatically – it could be a combination of these factors, which are not incompatible.

Resistance

As the intrusion of the uncanny phenomenon becomes more solid and insidious for the protagonist, their rational mind begins to exert a proportional force of resistance to deny it and preserve the dissociative structure that, until now, has allowed them to 'survive.' These are attitudes with a clear parallel in the psychology of trauma: at first, victims of traumatic experiences resist believing that it *is happening*, that it is happening to *them*, or that they must *respond to* the painful event. Denial, intellectualization, and rationalization are measures we all rely on to cope with the most primal and irrational parts of existence. In the face of chaos (that is, in the face of the traumatic, which attacks the axiomatic order of premises that order our vision of the world and of ourselves), these defensive strategies take on a special strength and rigidity. They are, on the other hand, defenses that rely on a certain logic of infantile magical thinking: *if I do not see it, it does not exist*; *if I deny its existence, it will cease to be in front of me*. It is a reaction very similar to that of a small child who covers their face when they see something frightening, in the hope that if they stop seeing it, it will no longer be there, it will no longer exist.

A paradigmatic example of denial can be found in the title of the film *Nope* (Peele, 2022). Faced with the obvious but inexplicable presence of a flying saucer, the protagonist – OJ – feels blocked, paralyzed, and simply mutters: "Nope." Interestingly, the film approaches trauma from several angles and characters: OJ has just suffered the unexpected and violent loss of his father, while the showman Jupe survived a murderous attack by a chimpanzee during the filming of a TV show as a child.

But denial of the phenomenon soon becomes unfeasible, and the protagonist's resistance becomes more nuanced: he admits that the event is real, but in no way accepts its supernatural nature, and sets out in search of rational explanations. Another example is found in *The Exorcist* (Friedkin, 1973). From Regan's first strange behaviors, her mother Chris does what any mother would do: she seeks diagnosis and the help of doctors. Even after seeing the girl's bed begin to shake spectacularly, Chris refuses to consider any supernatural explanation and leaves her daughter in the hands of doctors to undergo all sorts of tests. The director William Friedkin himself acknowledged that for many viewers the most shocking scene in the film is the arteriogram to which little Regan is subjected, and which was performed by real surgeons: the injection in the neck, the blood gushing like a fountain, the wince of pain. This sequence (like so many others of similar appearance in the horror canon) reminds us of some of the diagnostic or labelling operations performed on trauma victims, when they display some post-traumatic reactions. Examples include the reduction of such reactions to 'attention or hyperactivity problems;' the coercive responses exerted on children whose 'behavioral disturbances' are in fact the symptom of a post-traumatic organization; the praise and reinforcement of the over-adaptation or compulsive care to which other victims of interpersonal trauma resort; the negative interpretation (and consequent punishment) of the fragmentary behavior of so-called 'borderline' patients; etc. It is a set of interpretations which, in very different settings (clinical, school, cultural, institutional), reduces the traumatic dimension of behavior, and which is reminiscent of attempts *not to see* the supernatural threat (and the traumatic past that is sometimes associated with it) that we find in certain characters in horror fiction.

After another long series of tests, always shown as a process of torture, and a visit to a psychiatrist who will have no better luck with his attempt at hypnotism, the large committee of doctors first recommends the idea of exorcism (at 67 minutes into the film, i.e. the resistance has taken us past the halfway point), but they do so on the basis of the placebo effect: exorcism will only help the child to the extent that the child *believes* in the power of exorcism. As for the mother, she does not profess any kind of faith either, but at this point she is willing to try anything that will help her daughter.

We have already mentioned Annie, the protagonist of *Hereditary* and the method she uses to escape being colonized by her dead mother and to safeguard her sanity: making miniature models which recreate in extreme detail the most traumatic scenes of her family's past (Aster, 2018). This is a defensive mechanism very typical of psychosis or vulnerable or primitive psychological conditions: extreme dissociation. Annie needs to isolate these traumatic scenes on a scale she can control and in a format from which she can distance herself. Paradoxically, this strategy of Annie's produces a perverse effect on the way she relates to her real family: we could think that she is playing house with her children and husband, that she is turning them from subjects into objects. Defense mechanisms always have this paradoxical character: in the attempt to defend ourselves from something threatening, we indirectly provoke the threat (albeit in a different form) (Wachtel, 2014).

Annie's husband, Steve, embodies rational resistance to the insanity – symbolized by the demon Paimon and his followers – that wants to take over their house. His voice always pretends to be a dam of sanity against all delusional insinuations; he is against any kind of esoteric practice and even goes so far as to withhold information from his wife (the desecration of her mother's grave) in order to protect her emotional stability. Of course, all these attempts are doomed to failure, and the film unmistakably stages the precise moment when this last rational barrier collapses for Annie: when she throws her daughter's sketchbook into the fire, intending to free her family from madness/a curse, it is Steve who goes up in flames. With him, all sanity disappears, as we see in the sudden transformation of Annie's gesture: for her there is no more hope, chaos has triumphed, trauma has won.

Bol, the protagonist of *His House,* decides to deal with the first strange manifestations in the house his family have just moved into as if they were a simple problem of bad pipes and wiring, and consequently, the first place he turns to for help is the hardware section of a supermarket (Weekes, 2022). Eventually understanding the supernatural nature of the phenomenon (thanks to his wife, Rial, who never deludes herself), Bol's desperate strategy is to burn any items that can link them to the past and to the supposed curse (in the form of a monstrous witch) that haunts them as punishment for their sin: as we will learn at the end of the film, in their escape from Sudan they used a stray girl they passed off as their daughter, and later watched her die in the sea crossing. But while Rial is ready to face her own survivor's guilt head-on, Bol avoids it at all costs: he goes to buy a new suit, to reinforce his self-conviction that all is well, that their new life has already begun, and that all they have to do is behave like everyone else.

In *Jaws*, we also find another interesting resistance mechanism, which is the false culprit (Spielberg, 1975). A large tiger shark is caught by several fishermen in the village, and immediately everyone – including Brody – is ready to assume that it is the killer shark and that the problem has been solved. It is the scientist Hooper who, after making the appropriate measurements, raises the possibility that the animal is not responsible for the deaths. The search for a false culprit is an operation of displacement, a form of mental flight that consists of exchanging the frightening object. The real object is replaced by another, one more accessible to the imagination of the threatened person; in other words, a more powerful or more difficult object is abandoned for a less dangerous one.

No sheriff, no father: The dissolution of authority

One of the first realizations the protagonist of a horror film makes is that conventional authority is not competent enough to help him with his problem, starting with the police. The clumsiness of the officer on duty has become a quasi-comic trope of the genre, as demonstrated by the character of Deputy Dewey in the *Scream* saga (Craven, 1996). What this trope represents, obviously, is more than the inoperability of police authority in dealing with extraordinary phenomena. The sheriff embodies the order prior to the disruptive event, the normality (and normativity) on which the protagonists have built all their life assumptions. We could say that the policeman lacks not only the tools but also the 'jurisdiction' to intervene in the new symbolic order imposed by the event.

Even when it comes to investigators gifted with great insight, the subversive nature of the genre demands that they are never capable of solving the case and defeating the monster on their own: thus Detective Arbogast is killed just as he is about to discover Norman Bates' horrible secret in *Psycho* (Hitchcock, 1960), just as Sheriff Buster is killed by Annie Wilkes just as he discovers that she has locked writer Paul Sheldon in her basement in *Misery* (Reiner, 1990).

The disappearance of authority is often represented by the absence of the father figure, a familiar situation significantly prevalent in horror fiction. In *A Nightmare on Elm Street,* Craven fuses Nancy's (absent) father and the town sheriff into the same character: John Saxon (Craven, 1984). The script does not make it clear whether the original trauma (Krueger's lynching and mass murder) may have influenced the parents' separation, but it does emphasize the mother's inability to cope on her own, leading her to avoid and desensitize herself with alcohol. It is important to note that all the father's attempts to protect Nancy, in his dual role as policeman and father, are either futile or serve precisely to put his daughter in greater danger, such as his decision to barricade the windows of the house, condemning her to come face to face with Freddy. Similarly, in *Halloween* (Carpenter, 1978), it is interesting to note that it is Laura's own father who brings his daughter into confrontation with Myers in the first scene, by instructing her to leave keys at the entrance to an old, abandoned house; thus it is just by chance that the killer, who spies on her from inside, begins to obsess over her.

A failure of language

Perhaps the most important difficulty encountered by the protagonists of the genre when seeking help from any authority figure is the *impossibility of communicating* what is happening. At the core of the traumatic experience, as previously developed, is an experience of silencing. In the dialectic between saying and silencing that characterizes trauma, there is also the uselessness of the language of the community, with its symbolic categories and its maps of the world, to transmit the inexpressible Real that the subject is experiencing. In a certain way, it is a mutism reinforced by the lack of an appropriate language, and which requires complicated communicative maneuvers to overcome. Peak suggests:

> What we consider 'horror' fiction arises from this inability to communicate and is exemplified by two different types of narrative: 1) the narrative of the person with something to say that cannot be said (an inarticulate lucidity); and 2) the narrative of the person who is able to articulate his thoughts and emotions but still unable to make sense of his reality (an articulate confusion).
>
> (2014, p. 12)

An example of this confusion is found in *The Babadook* (Kent, 2014), when Amelia goes to the police station to try to report the harassment she is the victim of. The policeman's face shows not only disbelief, but something much worse: he looks at her as if *she* is the suspect in some crime. Everything Amelia says in her statement is true – the strange appearance of the children's book, the threatening phone calls – and correctly articulated, but it makes no sense to the policeman, who can only suspect her sanity.

We could even say that the real monster in the film is not The Babadook but the gaze of that big Other – to use the Lacanian term – which subjugates Amelia, and which is represented not only by the police, but also by the faculty of the school where her son Samuel studies, by her sister and the other mothers at her niece's birthday party, or even by the messages she receives from the television itself, where advertisements appear to reproach Amelia for not leading the romantic and happy life she should. This aligns with the kinds of emotions experienced by many victims of trauma: feelings of isolation, difference, stigmatization, and an overall sense of not belonging to the human community.

The impossibility of conveying a traumatic experience in words can lead, as we have seen, to all kinds of traumatic re-emergences that adopt different masks (flashbacks, dreams of repetition, etc.). A fascinating manifestation of this phenomenon, with which the horror narrative has played extensively, especially in the case of children, is the visual expression of their suffering through drawings. This phenomenon is documented in both child survivors of war and child victims of abuse, and horror fiction has picked it up in such profusion that one can almost speak of the trope of the 'child who draws horrible pictures.' We find it in *Insidious* (Wan, 2010), *Hereditary* (Aster, 2018), *The Ring* (Verbinski, 2002), *The Sixth Sense* (Shyamalan, 1999), *The Others* (Amenábar, 2001), *Sinister* (Derrickson, 2012), and many more.

The Babadook (Kent, 2014) offers an interesting variant, in that Amelia is an illustrator or author of children's stories (although she has not returned to work since her husband's death) and so it seems reasonable to think that she is herself the creator of *The Babadook* book, which supposedly *appears* on her son's bookshelf and then reappears when she destroys it. In this case, then, it would be the mother who unconsciously pours her trauma into the monstrous drawings. (That the book reappears despite having been destroyed reminds us of that *compulsion to repeat* that characterizes some traumas, and which we discussed in previous sections: the overpowering need of the traumatized mind to repeat the pain, to control or reprocess it).

Finally, it should be noted that other characters can perform this sanctioning function within the protagonist's story without needing to be invested with official authority. When Steven and Diane, the protagonist couple in *Poltergeist* (Hooper, 1982), begin to experience a series of strange manifestations in their house, they first turn to their neighbors, who have become representatives of absolute normality. The scene has a comical point even for Steven and Diane, who cannot even find the right words to explain what is happening to them. Hooper brilliantly introduces an apparently anecdotal element into the scene, the mosquitoes that attack the protagonists but leave the neighbors unharmed, as a symbol of the invisible barrier that separates the two couples in their perception of reality.

What happens in this kind of situation is that the protagonists are using unusable language, incomplete or full of wrong connotations, to refer to their new reality. This is the knot in which both the trauma victim and the character in the horror narrative find themselves tied when they perceive themselves to be involved in an irrational situation (when it is already undeniable): how to *say* what is happening? The first attempts are unsuccessful, as in the *Poltergeist* scene, and soon the victim recognizes that it is going to be very difficult, if not impossible, to make themself understood.

Acceptance

The "confirmation" stage, according to Carroll's terminology, comes when all attempts at rationalization have failed and the fantastic or extraordinary nature of the event is imposed. The protagonists accept that they are confronted with a new reality, for which they will need new tools and strategies; a phase of creative exploration and revision of frames of reference begins, where paths that until then seemed impassable, because of their absurdity, not only open up but are revealed as the only possible route.

On the essence of 'occult' fiction, Clover writes:

> Wherein lies the plot: convincing the White Science person of the necessity and indeed the superiority of Black Magic. The drama of these films thus turns on the process of conversion: the shedding of disbelief, the acceptance of the mystical or irrational.
>
> (2015, p. 67)

This is the moment when Regan's mother Chris decides to enlist the help of an exorcist to save her daughter's life (*The Exorcist*, Friedkin, 1973). Or when the mayor of Amity Island bows out and agrees to hire crazy old Quint to capture the great white shark (*Jaws*, Spielberg, 1975). Or when Steven and Diane decide to bring home the flamboyant medium Tangina (*Poltergeist*, Hooper, 1982). And so on.

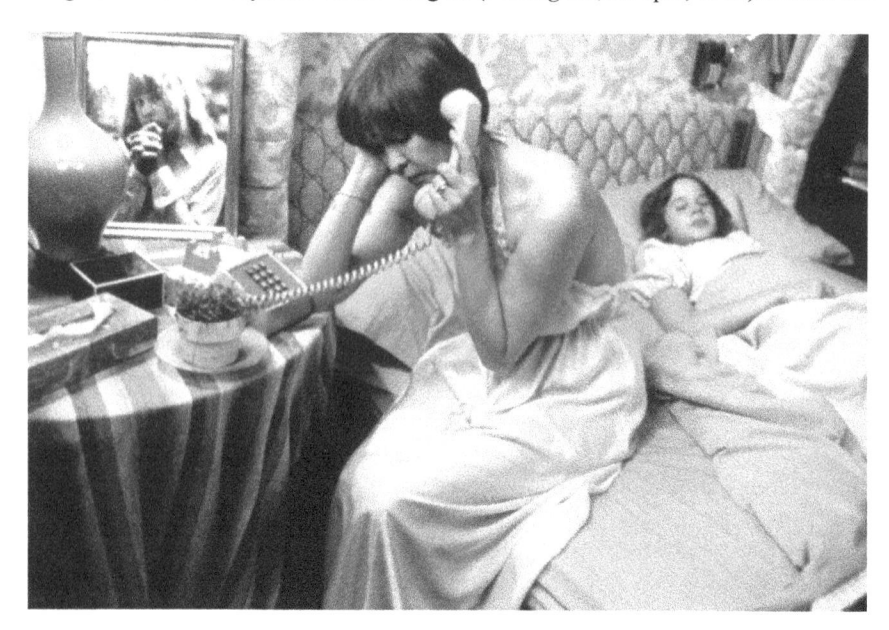

Figure 4.1 In *The Exorcist* (Friedkin, 1973), Regan's mother has to overcome all of her rational resistances and finally accept her need of another kind of help.

At this point in the terrifying event, therefore, the intervention of a new expert will become necessary; they will assume the role of the new authority (epistemological, fundamentally) in place of the failed conventional authority.

The role of the shaman

The medium or shaman is usually someone who has already gone through the same extreme experience as the protagonist. They embody the ideas of the initiate, the survivor, the war-maimed, the old madman, or the priest, and are always someone who lives on the margins of 'profane' society, since their soul or mental structure is already installed in another symbolic order. More important than magical skills, what the shaman brings is a new language to name and relate to the new reality. Hence the symbolic efficacy that Lévi-Strauss spoke of when he equated the function of the shaman with that of the psychoanalyst.

> The shaman provides the patient with a language in which immediate states that are unformulated and unformulable in any other way can be expressed. And it is the transition to this verbal expression (which allows, at the same time, to live in an orderly and intelligible form an actual experience that, without it, would be anarchic and ineffable) that causes the unblocking of the physiological process, that is to say, the reorganization, in a favourable sense, of the sequence whose development the patient suffers. In this respect, the shamanistic cure is halfway between our organic medicine and psychological therapies such as psychoanalysis. Its originality comes from applying a method very similar to the latter to an organic disturbance. [...] In both cases, the purpose is to bring to consciousness conflicts and resistances that have remained unconscious until that moment.
> (1966, p. 199)

The theatricality of the representations and strategies introduced by the medium (rituals or liturgical acts that materialize in fetishes, chants, legends, images, dances) thus connect with the Lacanian register of the imaginary, and also correspond to the diverse actions with which psychotherapy tries to offer opportunities for the articulation of experiences that have not been processed until now. This, which Bion understands as a transformation of raw experience into thought experience (1962), often involves the collaborative construction of a reflection or a new language in the consultation: patient and therapist are partners in thought (D.N. Stern, 2010). In the field of trauma-focused interventions, the use of artistic language, the incorporation of the body and its language, the use of narrative and storytelling, or the facilitation of a metaphorical language that gives voice to the dissociated parts after the trauma are examples of this search for a new language for trauma, and of this 'shamanic' function of the therapist.

As described in previous sections, the experience of trauma can be understood as the violent irruption of a hyper-concrete impact that cannot be understood with reason or articulated with language. In that sense, we speak of an assault of the

Real that dismantles our symbolic functioning (i.e. our logical, second-order processing, based on discrimination and a law of shared signifiers). The traumatized mind is presented with the problem of regaining some grip on reality through a new code, which allows it to understand and recover the ability to *say* something about what has happened. This is where the mediation of the shaman comes in, who, as has been said, presents the possibilities of the imaginary. As opposed to the registers of the rational, the masculine, logic, and ideas, the character can only confront the traumatic/unknown/monstrous in the realm of the visual, emotional, feminine, telluric, pre-logical, corporeal, and so on. We might think, then, that what is taking place at this point in the narrative – the intervention of the medium, with their new code for interpreting the world – is a *knotting* between the three registers (Real, symbolic, imaginary), which had been disarticulated as a result of the emergence of that disruptive traumatic real. This represents a shift where the disarticulated (and terrifying) Real is transferred – on the back of an imaginary support – to a new symbolic order in which the trauma can be signified and reintegrated.

It is not always necessary for a person to embody this shamanic function. Sometimes the protagonist gains access to new knowledge through an esoteric book or even (in lazy screenplays) a simple Google search.

In *The Evil Dead* (Raimi, 1981), a supposed copy of the *Necronomicon* serves the protagonists as a grimoire or ceremonial book to summon the spirits, although it offers no clues as to their ultimate dominion, so the characters are hopelessly doomed. In *Carrie* (De Palma, 1976), the main character learns the word "telekinesis" and all its implications from a simple library book.

In *Hereditary* (Aster, 2018), the real medium of the family is the grandmother, but since the film begins with her death, her role is replaced by that of a book (among her mother's things, Anne finds a volume entitled *Notes on Spiritualism*, where she will later find the name of the demon Paimon) and by the character of Joan, a mother traumatized by the loss of a child, who is willing to facilitate Anne's contact with her own recently deceased daughter through a seance.

In *The Vigil* (Thomas, 2019), Yakov is a young Jewish man going through a crisis of faith due to an unresolved trauma, but he agrees to act as a 'shomer' for one night, watching over the body of a recently deceased man. Besieged by shadows and strange occurrences, and physically trapped in the house, he descends into the basement, where a television shows a video of the late Rubin Litvak, a Holocaust survivor, explaining that he has spent his whole life running from a being who assaulted him in the forests of Buchenwald. Before Yakov's fascinated gaze, Litvak pronounces the name of the "*mazzik*" and describes them as "parasites" who attach themselves to "broken people," as demons with their heads turned backwards, condemned to always look at the past. Furthermore, he lays down the rules of this singular curse: the only way to get rid of the *mazzik* is to burn his "true face" the first night he appears; if Yakov has not done so by dawn, he will never get rid of him. In this way, we see how such a prosaic mechanism as a recorded video can perfectly fulfil this informing and orienting function.

In other fictions, it is the protagonist themself who develops shamanic powers: this happens when they go through a near-death experience in the early part of the story. According to Eliade says:

> The primitive magician, the medicine man or the shaman is not only a sick person: he is, above all, a sick person who has healed, and who has healed himself. Often, when the shaman's vocation manifests itself through an illness or an epileptic attack, the candidate's initiation is equivalent to a cure. [...] In all these examples, we encounter the central theme of an initiation ceremony: the dismemberment of the neophyte's body and the renewal of his organs; ritual death followed by resurrection and mystical fullness. [...] All these rituals and tests have the same purpose: to forget the past life. That is why in many places the candidate, when he returns to the village after initiation, pretends to have lost his memory, and they have to teach him to walk, to eat and to dress. Usually, the neophytes learn a new language and take a new name. The rest of the community believes that the candidates, during their stay in the wilderness, are as if dead and buried, or that they were devoured by a monster or a god, and when they return to the village they are considered as apparitions.
>
> (19676, p. 40)

This is literally what happens to John Smith in *The Dead Zone* (Cronenberg, 1983). After a car accident that brings him to the brink of death and leaves him in a coma for eight months, not only does he find he has to relearn how to walk and barely recognizes the world around him, but he feels that everyone looks at him like a ghost or a resurrected person: even his girlfriend has moved on with her life, assuming that John was never coming back. In addition – and this is where his status as a shaman is revealed – John has brought back the gift of clairvoyance from the "beyond."

Naming the monster

Where does the need to name the monster come from? In many horror stories the word that identifies the creature could be considered a kind of non-name, since to the uninitiated it sounds like gibberish, a conjunction of syllables not quite articulated, almost like pre-language or a child's first attempts at language: the name The Babadook is the perfect example.

In *His House* (Weekes, 2022), the first step from the disjointed Real to the symbolic occurs when the wife, Rial, tells her husband the legend of the so-called 'apeth:' by naming them, the shadows, voices, birds, and noises that have been manifesting themselves in the house since their arrival acquire a concrete meaning, and the trauma can be processed. Although this does not mean that the threat disappears, from then on Bol shares his wife's serenity to some degree, because he is no longer afraid of the phenomena as inexplicable, but fears them for exactly what they represent: the guilt that haunts them over the death of the stray child they used to escape from Sudan. And, as noted above, this process of knotting is sustained by acts of a liturgical or ritual nature. This is why Bol simply lights a candle to invoke the witch from then on, a minor but purposeful gesture, rather than wasting his time tearing up the walls of the house in search of an impossible explanation.

These incomprehensible words that allude to the monster or the strange phenomenon often operate as an invocation, a coded key, or a gateway to the other world: for example, the "redrum" in *The Shining* (Kubrick, 1980), the "Satori" in *Hereditary* (Aster, 2018), the "Carcosa" in *True Detective* (Pizzolatto, 2014), the intriguing "Esseker" in *Mirrors* (Aja, 2008), or even the song *Jeepers Creepers* in the film of the same title (Salva, 2001).

This represents a kind of "liturgy of emptiness," as Han puts it, which is based on the absence of meaning or the excess of signifier:

> Magical spells also carry no meaning. They are, in a way, empty signs. That is why they seem magical, like doors leading to the void. Ritual signs cannot be attributed a univocal meaning either. That is why they seem mysterious.
>
> (2015, p. 42)

Both the name and the origin of the monster and the 'rules' that may serve to invoke or control it inevitably come from a self-referential narrative framework, a backstory with pretensions to popular folklore: this is how urban legends work. They are about past events, supposedly real and repeated enough times to form a pattern or sequence that can be passed on, almost always orally and discreetly, as a secret.

In the film *Candyman* (directed by Bernard Rose [1992] and based on the story *The Forbidden* by Clive Barker [1985]), Helen is a young urban legend researcher who learns the story of the Candyman, a specter armed with a lethal hook that materializes before anyone who invokes his name five times in front of a mirror. The Candyman's actual existence depends exclusively on the community's belief in him; there is no ontological difference between being and being named, as the character himself admits: "I am what is written on the wall, what the children whisper in the classroom. Without that, I am nothing."

This viral power is also exemplified in *Slender Man* (White, 2018), where orality is replaced by the internet, given that it is a legend amalgamated from testimonies of uncertain origin shared in online forums (this type of story is known as a 'creepypasta,' a term derived from the copy and paste technique that defines them). In this film, not only do we see how the protagonists find out who the 'Slender Man' is on the internet, but also how they can invoke him by clicking on the link entitled "Invocation."

In the excellent *Under the Shadow* (Anvari, 2016), Shideh is a mother who stays with her young daughter in a building in central Tehran, under siege from bombs and strange ghostly presences, after her husband has marched to the front. Here the shamanic function is divided between a deaf-mute child in the neighborhood, who begins to speak of the presence of *djinn* (genies) in the building, and a book where Shideh finds the key to understanding what these spirits are. According to the belief, the genies ride on the wind. And in a subtle way their defeat is linked to overcoming one's own personal weaknesses: "Where there is fear and anxiety, that is where the winds blow."

Trance

O'Bannon (O'Bannon & Lohr, 2013) calls the turning point that brings us into the third act the point of no return. It occurs when the course of events has already acquired such inertia that, whatever the protagonist does, the final confrontation is already inescapable. In horror films, this moment is often accompanied by the realization that the protagonists are not adequately prepared for the fight – something inevitable, since by definition they are always characters facing a threat that is beyond them. It is the "You're gonna need a bigger boat" moment in *Jaws* (Spielberg, 1975), or the scene in *Alien* where Ripley asks Ash how they can defeat the monster and the android replies, simply: "You can't" (R. Scott, 1979).

The final confrontation between the protagonist and the monster, therefore, is always posed as an unequal combat, where the hero's chances of success are almost nil. We often see the protagonist engage in absurd, bizarre strategies, clearly destined to fail, such as OJ's plan to hunt down the flying creature in *Nope* (Peele, 2022). These are, however, not random strategies, but based on the knowledge the protagonist has acquired throughout the story, often with the help of the shaman. However, their character is more liturgical or ritualistic than rational, as we have seen; from our analysis, the magical efficacy of these strategies has to do with what they demonstrate in terms of overcoming and coping with one's own emotional conflicts.

In other words, it is precisely the precariousness of the protagonist's means and his disadvantaged position *vis-à-vis* the monster that provides the transformative value of his decision to confront it.

Consider what happens in *A Nightmare on Elm Street* (Craven, 1984): Nancy's boyfriend Glen fleetingly acts as a shaman when, before the third act, he lends her a small manual of guerrilla-style 'booby traps,' at the same time providing her with vaguely Eastern-inspired advice to lose her fear of Freddy: "You turn your back on him, take away his energy and he disappears." The traps Nancy sets against Freddy turn out to be completely ineffective in terms of physical struggle, but they serve an important function in strengthening her will and represent a crucial sign of change in her attitude. From a psychological point of view, the willingness to take concrete and real action to confront a problem, even more so if it is a new action, the outcome of which is still unknown, shows at the very least that the person has broken through the blockage and is brave enough to take a risk. This premise is at the core of some therapeutic proposals that integrate an introspective and insight-centered methodology (traditionally associated with psychoanalysis) with an approach centered on behavioral activation and overcoming, through concrete behavioral changes, cyclical patterns linked to insecurity and trauma (something associated with behavioral therapies). These approaches understand that knowledge about the internal dynamics underlying the patient's difficulties is often insufficient: in addition to knowing, the patient needs to do things, to get new, specific results in reality (see Wachtel, 1997). The undertaking of such seemingly 'silly' and doomed-to-failure strategies is a recurrent trope in the genre: we see it also in the pool scene of *It Follows*, already mentioned, when the protagonists devise a plan to catch the monster that can hardly work (Mitchell, 2014).

Trance occupies, in the narrative of cinematic horror, an important role in relation to the allegorical moments described in previous chapters. Recall that the allegorical moment represents the convergence of incompatible orders – the past and the present of the protagonist; the exterior, which has to do with the physical threat of the monster, and the interior, which has to do with the unresolved trauma of the protagonist; fantasy and the real, etc. – and, in turn, contains an important part of the emotional intensity of the trauma (as it re-emerges). In the moment of trance in some films, the coping actions that have been described (the renunciation of resistance, the acceptance of the supernatural character of the threat, the assumption of a new language for what is happening, etc.) converge to allow the protagonist to integrate, in some way, the previously insurmountable oppositions that were at the basis of the trauma. It is important to underline that this climactic moment always involves a physical action, a bodily commitment of the protagonist. This action has two movements that can be synchronous or successive: the voluntary surrender to (possible) sacrifice and the trapping of the monster.

A voluntary sacrifice: Turning your back on Freddy

"The crossing of the threshold is a form of self-annihilation," warns Campbell (1949, p. 77). The idea of death and resurrection that lies at the heart of the classical myth demands that the protagonist finally assume the role of sacrificial victim, willingly exposing himself to the monster in a gesture that must be more than a trick or a deception; it must effectively commit his life.

To explain the importance of this narrative movement, we can resort to a technical definition of the protagonist; for us, the protagonist is the character (or characters) upon whom the outcome of the story depends. In all kinds of stories, but especially in those that present extreme situations such as horror, the protagonist must assume responsibility for the decisive action, regardless of the fact that their initiative may also move other secondary characters to action or unleash opposing forces. As readers and viewers, we would not accept an outcome in which our hero succeeds due to someone else's merits; we would certainly prefer to see them fail in the attempt. In other words, the protagonist must be willing to take the greatest risk imaginable, must compromise his future (and often his life) in a final, voluntary decision.

This sacrificial offering as a paradoxical means of defeating the monster is made explicit in *A Nightmare on Elm Street* (Craven, 1984). In the final sequence, Nancy applies the advice given to her by her boyfriend and turns her back on Freddy, saying: "I take away all the energy I've given you. You are nothing." Nancy's surrender to Freddy's blades with absolute calmness is not only an act of contempt, but is in itself an overcoming of the fear that has gripped her throughout the film.

Figure 4.2 In the climax of *A Nightmare on Elm Street* (Craven, 1984), Nancy not only dares to confront Freddy Krueger directly, but she even turns her back on him to prove she is no longer afraid, thus nullifying his power.

It is, moreover, a form of coping in opposition to the repression that her parents and other adults applied fiercely after the traumatic events that led to Freddy's birth as a supernatural monster. Unaware of the intergenerational trauma she is inheriting, Nancy offers a response that, in its renunciation of rigid defenses, contains an opportunity for overcoming.

"You are nothing" are the exact same words Amelia uses when she comes face to face with the creature at the end of *The Babadook*, to which she adds: "This is my house! You are trespassing in my house! If you touch my son again I'll kill you!" It is worth noting that here there is a very important addition to Nancy's simple "You are nothing" or the "I am no longer afraid of you" of other films: Amelia – previously trapped in a strong emotional ambivalence towards Samuel – commits an act of reclamation of her son and her own motherhood, thus recomposing an affective bond that was being degraded by the trauma (and, in this case, by the monster that represents it).

In a similar way, at the end of *Alien* (R. Scott, 1979), Ripley turns her back on the monster as she dons her space-diving suit and sits waiting for the creature to come out of hiding, spurred on by the gas leaks. The moments that Ripley holds on without pressing the hatch button are the most agonizing in the film because, although we trust that our protagonist has a plan, we see how she in fact blindly exposes herself to the beast's advance from behind and is saved only by a few thousandths of a second.

This voluntary exposure has multiple variations and can be recognized, more or less explicitly, in almost every iconic horror film: Karras absorbing Regan's demon in *The Exorcist* (Friedkin, 1973), Hooper inserting himself into the flimsy cage in *Jaws* (not to mention Quint's death, or the very idea of capturing the immense shark with the meager "Orca") (Spielberg, 1975), Laurie staying in the house rather than fleeing with the children and literally turning her back on Myers in *Halloween* (Carpenter, 1978), Clarice showing up alone at the killer's house in *The Silence of the Lambs* (paradigmatically, here the idea of sacrifice is already included in the title) (Demme, 1991), etc.

Carrie (De Palma, 1976) is another example worth dwelling on. The monster/trauma that Carrie must confront and overcome is twofold: her social isolation (or rather, her branding as a freak) and the fanatical, emasculating domination she is subjected to by her mother, Margaret. In the film's long third act, Carrie decides to go to the prom in the company of Tommy, against her mother's wishes and knowing that this will mean exposing herself to the glares and unforgiving judgment of the very same classmates who hate and despise her. The humiliation of the bucket of blood dumped on her head at the moment of her coronation as prom queen signals that 'the monster' has indeed devoured her, and in that sense, it is a failure: her social fear is justified, and Carrie completes her transformation and identification with the freak that she is accused of being. After unloading her vengeance of fire and blood on the students and teachers at the school, she returns home in search of a meeting with her mother. "It was horrible, Mum. They laughed at me," she tells her, and takes refuge in her arms, surrendering like a child, even though her mother is absorbed in her grotesque sexual confession and keeps repeating that "the devil is back," clearly referring to Carrie. Rather than comfort Carrie, Margaret plunges a knife into her daughter's back. Badly wounded, Carrie falls down the stairs. As at the bloody party, there is no chance now for the mother's fanaticism to assimilate, overcome, or integrate and allow for a future for them both; Carrie unleashes her power and pins her mother to the wall, turning her into a parody of Jesus Christ. The failure is so resounding that the house begins to collapse, and Carrie takes refuge (with her mother's body) in precisely the same room where the mother would lock her up to pray, by way of punishment. This represents a regression to the deepest core of her trauma, and perhaps an act of total and definitive obedience to the persecutory introject that, by way of identification with the aggressor, has come to dominate Carrie's subjective experience. The house burns and collapses on them, sealing the tragedy and fusing them together definitively. This ending seems to partake of the same idea previously explored in *The Haunting* and *Psycho* (Hitchcock, 1960). In all these films, the object-internal-mother, despite the efforts of the son or daughter to differentiate and appropriate their own desire, ends up crushing and taking with it the protagonist's separate subjectivity.

Retrieve the body/Catch the monster

The body – the physical, real dimension, beyond words and symbols – is therefore the stage on which the final struggle with the enemy is enacted. In order to be in a position to expose oneself or surrender to the monster (with the intention of trapping it), it is essential to first regain control over one's own body.

In our psychological reading of fiction, this recovery is identified with the owning and integration of those traumatic emotions that, as we have seen, had been dissociated by a mind incapable of processing them. It has been observed that the experience of trauma can break the relationship between mind and body, fragment subjective life, or prevent the integration of mental functions that, in a healthy situation, operate harmoniously; many people affected by post-traumatic events learn to silence their emotions to the point of no longer knowing how to recognize them, and this has a direct reflection on how these emotions manifest themselves in the body (alexithymia). In a way, recovering the body and regaining control of the movements, expressions, and actions we perform with it, is a necessary step to recover the health of the mind. In the words of van der Kolk:

> Helplessness and immobilization keep people from using their stress hormones to defend themselves. When that happens, their hormones are still being pumped out, but the actions they're supposed to fuel are thwarted. Eventually, the activation patterns that were meant to promote coping are turned back against the organism and now keep fueling inappropriate fight/flight and freeze responses. In order to return to proper functioning, this persistent emergency response must come to an end.
>
> (2015, p. 339)

Van der Kolk then talks about his experience with body-based psychotherapies, where the history of what happened takes a back seat to exploring physical sensations and discovering the location and shape of the physical traces of past traumas. This path leads to a culmination of those impulses and "action tendencies" (protesting, attacking, calling for help, protecting oneself) that were stifled amidst the paralysis and silencing that occurs during trauma:

> Once patients can tolerate being aware of their trauma-based physical experiences, they are likely to discover powerful physical impulses—like hitting, pushing, or running—that arose during the trauma but were suppressed in order to survive. These impulses manifest themselves in subtle body movements such as twisting, turning, or backing away. Amplifying these movements and experimenting with ways to modify them begins the process of bringing the incomplete, trauma-related 'action tendencies' to completion and can eventually lead to resolution of the trauma.
>
> (2015, p. 340)

What van der Kolk proposes, in short, is to channel those frustrated tendencies to action through the conscious deployment of certain movements, and thus ensure that the body ceases to be a post-traumatic heterotopia in which unpredictable and painful manifestations are reproduced without control.

The first step in regaining control of the body, in the case of horror characters, is often to free themselves from some kind of physical bondage. If we think of Sally, the protagonist of *The Texas Chainsaw Massacre*, the last twenty minutes of the film are spent bound, in a sack, gagged, or tied to a chair, at the mercy of the depraved cannibal family (Hooper, 1974). Only at the last moment, just before being executed with a hammer, does Sally manage to break free from her captors and flee the house by throwing herself out of a window.

The eviction of the invading spirit is another way of recovering the body. We see it unequivocally in the case of the girl Regan (Friedkin, 1973), but also in the bloody vomit with which Amelia expels the Babadook from her body after the liberating caress of her son (Kent, 2014). It is the opposite of what happens in the aforementioned Carrie, on the other hand, where the protagonist girl succumbs to the destructive power that inhabits her body instead of freeing herself from it or learning to control it (De Palma, 1976).

Another example of a protagonist who tragically fails in his attempt to regain his body is Seth (played by Jeff Goldblum) in *The Fly* (Cronenberg, 1986). The whole film revolves around the story of how, after accidentally fusing his DNA with that of a fly, Seth's body is progressively emptied of humanity and replaced by pure animality (or, rather, by an abject animality, since he is a hybrid, a liminal creature between two natures).

When we speak of trapping the monster, we refer to the protagonists' efforts to draw the monster into the real world, to bring it out of its nightmarish realms and subject it to the reign of physical laws or, failing that (when the monster is irreducible to the norms of the physical reality we inhabit), to subject it to some kind of moral or psychological regulation. (The hero's willingness to sacrifice himself to save others implicitly serves as the first step in subjecting the monster to a genuinely human ethic.) In our analysis, this translates as bringing the trauma out of the unconscious and into consciousness, where it can be subjected to bodily and affective processing that would ultimately culminate in a narrative integration of the trauma.

The paradigmatic example is, again, *A Nightmare on Elm Street* (Craven, 1984), where Nancy's strategy is to embrace Freddy during sleep, to be immediately woken up (in the absence of her boyfriend Glen, she uses an alarm clock), and thus bring him into the waking world, the real world, where he can be defeated as a mortal man.

Even in a starkly realistic film like *The Texas Chainsaw Massacre*, we can interpret the denouement in this way: Sally manages to escape from the cannibals' house, which represents the pure core of irrationality and chaos, and runs until she reaches the nearby road, pursued by Leatherface and his brother (Hooper, 1974). The road is nothing but a symbol of civilization or rationality, so it is not surprising that the brother is run over by a truck and Sally escapes the lethal chainsaw by climbing onto the back of a passing van.

Another of the prosaic laws imposed by the natural realm (as opposed to the ghostly realms, say) is the need to feed, and so in the final scene of *The Babadook* we see Amelia and her son collecting bugs and worms in the garden of their house; the insects are the food that the mother will deposit in the basement where the creature now lives, still ferocious but domesticated, stripped of all its destabilizing power (Kent, 2014).

As we explained at the beginning, the altered perception of the passage of time is a typical characteristic of the way traumas are experienced and relived. This is why another of the usual strategies for trapping the monster consists of introducing it into a normal temporality, marked by a clock or a countdown. This happens in *A Nightmare on Elm Street*, when Nancy sets her alarm clock to go off in ten minutes (Craven, 1984), or in *Alien*, when Ripley activates the countdown to the destruction of the Nostromo ship (R. Scott, 1979).

In the case of ghosts, the first way to draw them into the physical and rational world is to entice them to manifest themselves in some way that can be interpreted or recorded by a video camera or other device. This happens in *Poltergeist* (the 'holy company' who descend the stairs of the house and are not seen by human eyes, but are recorded by cameras) (Hooper, 1982); *Paranormal Activity* (the whole film revolves around home video footage) (Peli, 2007); *The Sixth Sense* (the sound recording of interviews where ominous psychophonies are heard) (Shyamalan, 1999); and dozens more. In *The Changeling* (Medak, 1980), a whole paranormal panoply is deployed to communicate with the boy's ghost: not only is there a seance, where the voice of the specter is recorded on tape as a psychophony, but the medium performs a demonstration of psychography or automatic writing, immersed in a trance-like state.

In the denouement of *Nope* (Peele, 2022), filmmaker Holst dies and fails in his attempt to capture the flying creature with his hand-cranked camera. Once the creature has finally been destroyed, director Peele underlines the even greater importance of the seemingly trivial event that takes place next: Em manages to take a photograph of the creature at the last instant, proving its very existence.

In this sense, defeating the monster becomes synonymous with exposing it to the light, bringing it out of its dark zone; in our interpretation, it would be the first form of voluntary exposure to trauma, painful but necessary. The exposure of the monster to the light probably metaphorizes, in addition to a certain surrender or exposure to the hitherto dissociated pain, the reactivation of a reflexive process, an attempt at symbolization, the first steps towards integration. When Nancy embraces Krueger to take him to the other side, she is not only confronting her fears and disempowering the monster, she is leading him into the territory where these threats can be thought through without childish fantasy, anxious anticipation, shame, or helplessness interrupting the self-reflection and narrative effort that seeks to understand, communicate, and integrate (Craven, 1984).

The triumphant smile of trauma

It is undeniable, in any case, that from the 1960s onwards the horror genre has had a certain inclination towards bleak or "disaffirmative" endings, in Holland-Toll's terms (2001). As we will develop later in this book, the overcoming or 'embrace of the monster' endings have acquired significant prominence during the last two decades, but nevertheless, we still find an abundance of titles that bet on a pessimistic outcome in the protagonist's struggle with his monster-trauma.

Perhaps the most obvious example is provided by the blockbuster *Smile* (Finn, 2022), one of the films that has most explicitly placed trauma at its narrative core in recent years. The protagonist, Rose, is a psychotherapist caught in a chain of deaths caused by an entity that literally "feeds on trauma." Rose's involvement is not accidental, as she struggles to heal her own traumatic wound: her mother's suicide before her very eyes when she was just a child. It is a memory almost identical to the one that haunts the protagonist of another recent genre hit: *Talk to Me* (Philippou & Philippou, 2022). In both cases, the protagonists' conflicts with the monstrous representations of their mothers ends in gruesome defeat.

Hereditary (2018) and *Midsommar* (2019) have established Ari Aster as one of the most personal and evocative voices in horror fiction in recent years. Although they are very different narratives, the director himself has acknowledged that there is a symmetry between them. The oppressive darkness of *Hereditary* is transformed into open luminosity in *Midsommar*, and the horror of the family becomes the horror of the community, but both share the same final climax in the form of a coronation ceremony. The crown, like the nimbus around the head, is symbolically associated with divinity, victory, overcoming, transmutation, and spiritual evolution. The triumphant hero returns from the underworld endowed with a power/treasure in the form of knowledge that elevates him above others and connects him to a higher level of consciousness. What we witness in *Hereditary* and *Midsommar*, however, is the crowning of two completely alienated people. Peter, the boy traumatized by the death of his sister in *Hereditary*, is crowned by the priestess of the cult when, after fleeing his own mother's diabolical attack, he has already lost all capacity for reason and his body is definitively taken over by the spirit of Paimon. The last shot of the film, with the discomposed expression on his face, the cardboard crown (inherited from his sister's corpse) on his head, and his broken nose, leaves no doubt: Peter is a hopelessly deranged being.

The end of *Midsommar* has lent itself to some controversy because Dani's final smile, as she watches the flames where her boyfriend and the rest of the sacrificed are being consumed, can be understood as a gesture of liberation. And no doubt it is. But it is a liberation in the form of an escape or a fall into madness; the girl has definitively cast off her ties with reality, deserting any struggle to come to terms with her trauma, to immerse herself in the fantasy constructed by the pagan community. Lest there be any doubt as to the director's intentions, let us look at an extract from the last page of the original script:

> On the upward LIFT, we cut to a tight CLOSE-UP of Dani's face. She is being carried forward. Her expression, which begins as one of great distress, slowly starts to TURN. Her agony subsides into sudden CONFUSION. What's happening? Where am I? I'm on this chair, being carried! Her expression goes from FEAR to EXCITEMENT to CONFUSION again. She suddenly lets out an abrupt LAUGH (which we can't hear over the music and the now-deafening FIRE).

Dani is now being taken over by an invading sense of pride and contentment. This soon evolves into a manic exhilaration. Dani BEAMS. She has been embraced by a new family. She is Queen. She is not alone. A SMILE finally breaks onto Dani's face. She has surrendered to a joy known only by the insane. She has lost herself completely, and she is finally free. It is horrible and it is beautiful. CUT TO BLACK.

(Aster, 2017; pp. 116-117)

Dani's smile has a chilling similarity, in this sense, to the smile that appears on the faces of *Smile*'s victims when they are hopelessly possessed by the trauma-entity. As the film's tagline says, "Once you've seen that smile, it's too late."

And, from a psychological point of view, it is not difficult to understand the temptation to remain suspended in a state of inner trance when reality only offers a continuous cycle of pain, guilt, and impotence. This is the case for Dani, who, as discussed in previous sections, faces not only an experience of traumatic loss but also an indifferent response from her environment. A complex traumatic solution is thus configured that makes it unbearable for the protagonist to remain in the world.

Here, therefore, is presented the most difficult and also the most important step in the process of overcoming trauma: the leap "from the inner dream space to the outer real space; the transition from the sphere of the unconscious to that of consciousness, from the call in the dream to the call to action, from traumatic repetition to ethical responsibility" (Pérez, 2018, p. 126).

As an Upanishad quoted by Joseph Campbell says: "Who, having abandoned the world, would wish to return again? He only desires to be there" (Campbell, 1949).

Figure 4.3 At the end of *Midsommar* (Aster, 2019), Dani's face turns from a pained grimace to an unhinged smile: far from signifying a triumph or an overcoming, this smile suggests a definitive fall into the abyss of trauma.

'Being there' sometimes manifests itself, in fact, in an expression of deranged glee. In addition to the grimace of Dani (Aster, 2019) and the victims in *Smile* (Finn, 2022), we can also think of Norman Bates' half-smile in the last shot of *Psycho* (Hitchcock, 1960), or Thomasin's expression when she joins, literally floating in ecstasy, the final coven of *The Witch* (Eggers, 2016), or Sally's hysterical laughter when she jumps into the trailer in the denouement of *The Texas Chainsaw Massacre* (Hooper, 1974). It is unimaginable that any of these people could lead a 'normal' life after this moment of total rupture with sanity. They are characters who, in their contact with different aspects of the traumatic, have been absorbed in their transit through this 'other side.'

Chapter 5

Reclaiming the metaphor, embracing the monster

Using horror films in psychotherapy with traumatized patients

Trauma occurs when a painful and dangerous event (or series of events) overwhelm an individual's capacity to integrate their emotional experience, stimulating hyperactivation states and subcortical defenses (i.e., automatic, procedural) that can become chronic (Dent, 2020). Damages experienced by trauma victims are often compounded by environmental indifference, victim stigmatization, lack of recognition of injustice, or narrative distortions (see Dent, 2020; Herman, 2015; Koren-Karie, Oppenheim, & Getzler-Yosef, 2008; Atwood & Stolorow, 2014), which further contribute to the aforementioned compromises in thinking, communicating, and integrating what happened. In these conditions, emotional pain is registered more at the procedural than at the semantic level, closer to the body than to words (Dent, 2020; Hill, 2015). Later, unsuccessful attempts to understand or communicate one's suffering through words can have the retraumatizing effect of shame (Hill, 2015) or a chronic sense of social isolation.

As stated in previous chapters of this book, the underlying logic of our daily processing of experience is "metaphor" or analogy (Modell, 1997; Modell, 2005; Modell, 2009). We derive the meaning of what happens to us by comparing the present with the past. This comparison is bidirectional: we also re-transcribe the meaning of past experiences in light of present events. Our psyche is constantly engaged in an implicit (and largely preverbal) conversation that looks back to project us forward. Trauma has the capacity to interrupt these metaphorical processes. In terms of the Predictive Processing Framework (PPF), trauma exposes us to excessive volatility and prediction errors that can be very difficult to reduce using our existing priors (Kube et al., 2020). Our daily metaphors are revealed as insufficient in the face of the excess of novelty and the affective overload that trauma provokes; we feel that we have lost references, and that some of our core assumptions about the world have been shattered (Janoff-Bulman, 1992).

We believe that the materials provided by modern horror films can help patients reclaim their metaphoric abilities. Horror cinema possesses a special richness of visual and auditory resources aimed at provoking intense affective reactions (Clasen, 2017), representing the unconscious, or showing us ways (which sometimes seem impossible or unlikely) in which humans can overcome very intense fears. Thus, these films may be privileged tools for facilitating free association around difficult content, formulating dissociated affects, exploring core conflicts and contradictions associated with the post-traumatic experience, or thinking about healthier forms of post-traumatic coping, among other uses.

The present chapter aims to explore some possible uses of imagery and metaphors from modern horror cinema in integrative therapeutic work with patients who have suffered trauma. Clinical experience shows us that it is advisable to employ methods alternative to words to access trauma-related content. Art and its manifestations may be one such method. However, to our knowledge, addressing trauma through the specific use of horror films has barely been studied, with a few valuable exceptions (Hamilton, 2020; Hamilton & Sullivan, 2015; Knafo, 2020).

Three approaches to the use of horror films in psychotherapy

According to Wolz, there are various ways to use film material in psychotherapy processes (2010). Three of the ways suggested by the author are especially relevant to our understanding of the possible use of horror films in working with traumatized patients.

The "evocative way" consists of spontaneously exploring the client's emotional responses and fantasies around films, and using these reactions in a manner analogous to dream work (Wolz, 2010). Certain films, scenes, or characters can particularly move patients, indicating that these likely represent material with emotional relevance. This usually takes the form of spontaneous comments such as: "I saw a film last week, and it made an impression on me" or "I just remembered a scene from this film that used to scare me very much when I was little." From this perspective, our work could consist of facilitating free association around these filmic materials, resonating with their possible unconscious meanings from our evenly hovering attention, or collaboratively unraveling the implicit meanings that the cinematic metaphor conveys. It is expected that within this framework – which facilitates a more spontaneous and creative conversation around previously stuck content – new, richer, and more articulated emotional responses may unfold (the subject of the second way, which we explore below).

The "cathartic way" helps clients access stored, unexpressed, and unformulated emotions, and release them (Wolz, 2010). This can accelerate the healing process, while stimulating the unfolding of "transformational affects" (Fosha, Thoma, & Yeung, 2019), such as 'mastery' affects (related to being able to connect with and survive emotions that were previously threatening); 'tremulous' affects (such as curiosity/interest associated with the emerging process of change); or 'enlivening' affects (such as excitement, exuberance, or zest for exploration), among others. Peri- and post-traumatic dissociation, or freezing that prevents victims from deploying help-seeking, attack or flight responses, operate against affective processing. Against paralysis of body and mind (Levine, 2010), and against dissociation (Schore, 2021), reconnecting with one's own emotional response in the safe material of a film can stimulate very relevant change processes.

The "prescriptive way" involves actively introducing work around specific films with the aim of stimulating new (more productive) ways of thinking and modeling healthy behaviors in the client (Wolz, 2010). Here, the film material becomes the object of a more focused and systematic work than in the previous models. In Wolz's words":

> [l]istening to stories and watching movies in a focused way create a form of trance state, similar to the state often achieved via guided visualizations. This kind of trance work is designed to help clients get in touch with a mature and wise part of themselves that helps them overcome problems and strengthen positive qualities.
>
> (2010, pp. 206-207)

This approach would try to help patients overcome some of the paradoxical effects of post-traumatic defenses and interpersonal protective strategies: they make victims more vulnerable to re-traumatization, social isolation, increased PTSD symptoms, etc. (Ehlers & Clark, 2000; Wachtel, 2014). Systematic work aimed at expanding the patient's horizon of possibilities constitutes an indicated strategy for trauma-focused work.

Our proposal for trauma-focused work with horror films moves between the three approaches just described (Wolz proposes a fourth way, called "cinema coaching," which we do not include in our model), and incorporates specific tools that we describe in the following pages.

Iconic language and formulation of experience

Horror cinema, with its mix of images, sounds, music, and the emotionally intense expression of actors, is particularly suitable for accessing emotional content that has been excluded from awareness, due to the bilateral disconnection affecting the traumatized brain (Chong, 2015). The archetypal images (powerfully crafted by cinematic artistry) of ghosts, haunted houses, hidden zones of the domestic space, dark forests, bodies coming to life, broken mirrors, possessed bodies, etc., have an evocative power that is likely above what other cinematic subgenres offer.

The very language of horror is often analogous to core aspects of traumatic phenomenology. Some patients say they feel "haunted" by sensations, memories, and emotions; there are 'hidden things' and 'dark places' that patients refuse to visit. Monk states that survivors of interpersonal trauma often perceive themselves and the world from a "curse position," a persistent feeling of being victims "of a disproportionate amount of bad luck yet could never account for why this was the case [and which usually becomes] a self-fulfilling prophecy" (2023, p. 1).

Parallelisms between the symbols of horror films and post-traumatic pain serve as potential reactivators of metaphor. This suggests that, for some patients, horror narratives could function as a reflective mirror, either through free association (as Wolz's evocative method suggests) or through more structured approaches (cathartic or prescriptive methods). These narratives provide a source of images and words to articulate the unspeakable aspects of their experiences.

This concept aligns with Hobson's assertion (cited in Barkham et al., 2016) that symbols and metaphors are essential elements in therapeutic conversations. Such elements are particularly relevant when patient and therapist collaborate to co-create deep "emotional knowing." This form of knowing involves representational symbols (i.e., emotions linked to imaginative ideas) that render the patient's affective experience significant, accessible, and tolerable. In this therapeutic context, images, cultural content, novels, films, and art are fundamental tools. A well-known anecdote recounts Hobson recommending Conrad's *The Heart of Darkness* to a psychiatry student seeking to understand depression, rather than relying solely on his extensive technical knowledge of the disorder.

Symbols present in films can thus be vital sources for negotiating emotional meaning between patient and therapist. This shared elaboration fosters an understanding that is direct and holistic, rather than fragmented and analytical. It is a creative exchange that offers new access to the inner worlds of patients. Herein lies the power of iconic (cinematic) symbols:

> Symbols enable people to elaborate 'inner forms'; conceptions which can be modified, combined, re-combined in the process of thinking and solving problems. Figurative speech, which involves symbolic language and metaphor, has a sense of movement and direction: There is a sense of layered meanings and complex connections.
>
> (Barkham et al., 2016, p. 8)

The spontaneous appearance of film material can occur both in the patient's and the therapist's mind. Wedding and Niemiec (2003), for example, describe how, during the treatment of a very depressed man, and upon hearing the patient talk about his feelings of emptiness, the therapist had a spontaneous memory of the protagonist of *Fight Club* (Fincher, 1999), a character trapped in a mechanical and empty life. The therapist shared this mental image, which was followed by a conversation about the film and the protagonist's need to create an imaginary alter ego.

Through discussing conflicts or scenes contained in horror cinema, some repudiated aspects of experience could achieve a greater degree of formulation (D.B. Stern, 2013). Consider sexual abuse, as an example. The contents involved in this trauma (memories, sensations, adult sexual impulses, the possibility of experiencing pleasure in any form, etc.) may have been defensively excluded behind the barriers of dissociation and numbness. For these patients, talking or feeling anything connected to the trauma is impossible; phenomenologically, the trauma is a kind of empty place. In such a case, discussing films like *Repulsion* (Polanski, 1965) or *Gerald's Game* (Flanagan, 2017), where different aspects of the psychic aftermath of sexual abuse are depicted, could reactivate a type of symbolic processing, and part of the analogical *game* involved in the metaphorical processing described by Modell (1997; 2005; 2009).

Cinema offers a dual experience of immersion and distance that makes it a powerful vehicle for working through trauma, especially when other more "cortical" forms of processing (such as reflection or abstract language) are inaccessible to the traumatized patient (Hamilton, 2020; Hamilton & Sullivan, 2015). Thanks to the power of the visual, the metaphor, and the creative (and pleasurable) use of ambiguity, horror films help re-establish the capacity to play with the contents of an unprocessed experience, reconnect with one's own pain with a sense of control, observe one's experience reflectively, construct (collaboratively) a meaning for it, or deliberate on more adaptive coping methods.

Moving within the window of tolerance

One of the principles of working with trauma is to expose patients to post-traumatic affects in tolerable doses, within a setting that allows them to control the rhythm, intensity, and cycles of activation–deactivation (Dent, 2020; Hill, 2015). This applies to the recollection of specific traumatic scenes, contact with core emotions that have not previously been expressed, or even the degree of intimacy and dependence experienced within the therapeutic relationship (Liotti, 2011). Moving within a window of tolerance (Dent, 2020) helps patients (re)process trauma-related affects but also – perhaps more importantly – gain a sense of affective competence that they have lacked. The recovery of agency, the feeling that the internal world – filled with terrifying 'monsters' – is more understandable and tolerable than previously thought, or the knowledge of interoceptive signals that indicate the potential for dysregulation, all contribute to rebuilding a sense of security within individuals regarding their inner world. These considerations are pertinent for work consistent with the cathartic way proposed by Wolz (2010). As a preliminary step for this work, it is advisable to establish the foundations of a safe experience, which involves, for example, a therapeutic relationship based on protective boundaries, or the management of neuro-biological stress responses (Hamilton & Sullivan, 2015).

Therefore, the resources offered to therapists by horror films must be used with special sensitivity to the emotional and interpersonal vulnerability derived from our patients' traumatic experiences. Too much intensity can confirm the patient's belief that they lack agency over their affective world. Too many words can inadvertently collude with the dissociative defenses of some patients; too few words can lead to a re-transcription of the experience at the procedural/bodily level. A therapist–patient relationship too focused on solutions may inadvertently convey the message that there is something wrong with the patient (or represent another failure in recognizing pain and bearing witness to injustice) (Benjamin, 2017; Herman, 2015); on the contrary, a relationship excessively charged with affect can feed the patient's feelings of dependency or load the therapeutic process with contraindicated toxicity (Dent, 2020). In all cases, we must avoid one-size-fits-all approaches, and protect a process that oscillates between emotional surrender and a sense of control over the rhythms and intensity of emotions.

In many modern horror films, although trauma is integrated into the circuit of symbolization (see later in this chapter for an explanation), it does not fully penetrate the ordinary experience of the characters. The monsters are integrated and, at the same time, remain separated by a mental or physical distance that allows the characters to resume their personal development. Traumatic resolution in these films is a matter of *connecting, but not too much*. For instance, the monster in *The Babadook* ends up occupying a space halfway between the conscious lives of the characters and the well-sealed basement, where mother and son descend for a short time each day to feed it and, perhaps, to remember that it exists. This reminds us of Volkan's description of "objects of mourning" (2018). According to this author, the photo of the deceased, the cemetery, the memorial, etc., function as spaces where grief can be reactivated, processed, and – most importantly – deactivated. These objects give agency to the person by allowing them to open and close the reflective process at will. They also provide security by locating the trauma within a domain bounded by the limits of ritual and certain symbolic and physical boundaries.

Moving in the transitional space

Upon these foundations of safety, work with horror cinema materials can facilitate gradual approaches to core traumatic affects. In Winnicottian terms, this work may allow patient and therapist to develop a conversation more akin to *play* than direct (and potentially excessive and painful) access to the reality of the trauma. For Winnicott, culture and art constitute "transitional phenomena" par excellence, the forms of play that adults use (1953). Transitional phenomena grant the child (and the adult) a space halfway between the illusion of omnipotence and the demands of adapting to reality. For work with traumatized individuals, moving in a transitional zone implies approaching the passivity, helplessness, or senselessness of the traumatic experience while retaining a sufficient degree of control and maintaining a protective omnipotent fantasy: "Art can provide a 'transitional space' to 'externalize' a concrete representation of trauma experience and discussion of artwork can enable meaning and sequence to be attached through constructing a narrative" (Hamilton, 2020, p. 4). Thus, filmic tropes and images may allow traumatized individuals to move transitionally: talking about a personal fear as if it were (in part) foreign; talking about something inside oneself as if it were (also) outside; being exposed to a previously passively experienced situation from a position of control; externalizing internal psychic material in the shared space of therapeutic conversation; turning the rigid material of trauma into the more plastic material of shared cultural play (between patient and therapist).

Conversation in the transitional space, around the images provided by cinema and under the form of play, can help patients reclaim metaphor. By examining characters and monsters in films (and the fear they provoke), the patient is playing at talking about themselves while talking about others and, for the first time, is outside of their conflict (but not defensively excluding it, they are exploring it from a new place). As in any playful dynamic, there is a double consciousness: being inside the game (and believing what one is talking about: "That character truly has reasons to be scared!") and being outside of it (implicitly, the patient *knows* they are exploring and wondering about the reasons for their fear). This continuous (and fragile, as it can be lost in traumatic reabsorption or under dissociative disconnection) interplay is the essence of the thirdness (Benjamin, 2017) we aim to achieve in therapy. As Danielle Knafo suggests:

> Cinema introduces a 'third' in the therapeutic relationship, an object that is outside the treatment space, but is brought into the treatment space. […] Because there is a shared dimension in the emotions expressed, it is safer for patients, and therapists, to engage with them.
>
> (2020, p. 1518)

Consider how an adult going through traumatic grief could benefit from a conversation around horror films like *Don't Look Now* (Roeg, 1973) or *The Changeling* (Medak, 1980). In both films, the protagonist is a grieving father and the film is set after the accidental death of their child; in both, the difficulty of moving forward and resolving their grief manifests as a ghostly return of the child. A parent's complicated grief, in its capacity for devastation and absorption, could prevent the person from thinking or talking about these ambivalences: the adult is simply *in* their pain. The world is tinged with loss, and everyone else (spouses, colleagues, friends, or the therapist) are characters in that rigidly unfolding drama. Reflection on how the horror of encountering the child's ghost is mixed with the hope of seeing them again could help reactivate the patient's reflective capacities. Saying goodbye is necessary, but dangerous at the same time (something that explains the "fixation" on the deceased also found in other films, such as *Godsend* [Hamm, 2004], *Bram Stoker's Dracula* [Coppola, 1992], or *The Skin I Live In* [Almodóvar, 2011]. Reflecting upon films like these, patients may begin to look from a new place (a "third" place) at the emotional knot in which they are stuck.

These considerations about the (seemingly) contradictory mix between wishing to be close to the deceased and saying goodbye to resolve grief connect to a broader problem affecting trauma victims: the subjective convergence of fantasy and reality, past and present, inner and outer world, etc. The traumatized mind is a mind traversed by paradox and, as we explore in the following section, terror has a fundamental resource to approach such paradox.

Allegorical moment and the transition from dissociation to conflict

As has been exposed in previous chapters, one of the aspects that makes trauma very difficult to process is that, often, traumatic experience (particularly, relational trauma) is contradictory and disjointed. Trauma escapes daily logic that distinguishes between past–present, inside–outside, emotion–action, or fantasy–reality. For the traumatized person, the familiar is simultaneously dangerous, the homely becomes suddenly un-homely. Significant others can be sources of love and care and, at other times (in an unpredictable and uncontrollable way), become dangerous figures. Institutions and authorities are the only place to turn to for protection, but often they display responses that – by omission – side with the aggressors (see Herman, 2015). Therefore, the distinctions that sustain our maps of the world can become blurred (something that also frequently happens in horror stories [Clute, 2006]), and the sense of self is stuck between contradictory representations: feeling good and bad, victim and aggressor, worthy and unworthy, capable and helpless, etc. (see Karpman, 1968). Contradictions associated with trauma can stimulate a fragmentation of the mind: victims may use different feeling and behavior policies that alternate abruptly and without continuity (Bromberg, 2011; Caligor et al., 2018; Liotti, 2011).

All of this implies that trauma can only be represented with an aesthetic that is ambiguous and escapes categorization: the aesthetic of horror cinema (Lowenstein, 2005). In horror films, this ambiguity condenses in what the author calls the "allegorical moment," a moment that involves a rupture of the binary categories with which we rationally organize reality: dead–alive; inside–outside; fantasy–reality; past–present. As described earlier, the well-known scene from *Psycho* in which Lila Crane descends into the basement of Norman Bates' house is one of the most popular allegorical moments in the horror canon (Hitchcock, 1960). In this sequence, our mind is confused: Norman's mother is dead (she is a preserved body in a chair, as we have just discovered), but she is not entirely dead because, otherwise, how could she also be in the doorway? The 'living' elderly woman (the one approaching Lila with the knife) is actually Norman himself, dressed in his dead mother's clothes and hair. The identification with the aggressor (Frankel, 2002) has reached its maximum expression: Norman's mind is confused with the introject of his abusive and suffocating mother. Instead of symbolically relocating his dead mother (for example, as a memory or a portrait), Norman has *become* his mother.

This scene metaphorically expresses the intense ambiguity surrounding attachment trauma, where interpersonal contradictions and psychological violence have been so intense that there is a failure of self-differentiation and psychological boundaries between the victim and the aggressors (who are often primary attachment figures). Material like this could facilitate therapeutic discussion of such ambiguities, the difficulty some patients have in distancing themselves from the internal voice of their aggressive introjects, or the automatic and invasive appearance of dissociated self-states (experienced as "not-me") that sometimes take control of the patient's subjective experience and behavior.

More generally, our proposal is that the reactivation of the metaphor can often concentrate around these allegorical moments in horror films. The imagery of horror cinema seems particularly useful for this purpose because it abounds in tropes marked by ambiguity, approach-avoidance, and fascination-fear conflicts, or moments where irreconcilable categories (past–present; fantasy–reality; dead–alive) are simultaneously expressed. Recurrent, playful conversation around these discrepancies can facilitate a therapeutic movement that takes patients from the dissociative solution (based on maintaining separate parts as irreconcilable) to a position based on conflict (Bromberg, 2011), where the mind can simultaneously hold two opposing tendencies (for example, the desire to separate from the internal representation of a castrating mother, and the simultaneous desire to stay close to her for safety and cohesion).

Embracing the monster: Identification and reappropriation of trauma-related contents

Film critic Andy Crump argues that some representative films of modern horror cinema follow a logic he calls "embracing the monster" (2020). In more traditional forms of horror, the monster "is usually either overcome or victorious by the end of the movie. The protagonist struggles, and wins or loses," the author writes. But horror is elastic, and there exists a recent strain of the genre where "the monster, in whatever form it takes, isn't bested but in some way accepted. Characters embrace it instead of fighting tooth and nail against it." For Crump, the climax of these stories is not based on the destruction of the threat but on its *assimilation*: what initially seemed like an external pursuer is accepted as an intrinsic element of personal experience, a part of one's own personal history. The success of the adventure lies in re-appropriating those unrecognized aspects of oneself that the monster represents, in understanding the meaning of the threat and allowing oneself to be transformed by it.

Again, a paradigmatic example of this logic is found in *The Babadook* (Kent, 2014), which centers around a mother who lost her husband the same day she gave birth to their son. The confluence of the son's birth with the husband's death stimulates, in addition to traumatic grief, a complicated mix of love and rejection towards this son who has become associated with the mother's misfortune. The eponymous monster in the film represents the woman's unformulated grief and hatred that, throughout the film, tries to invade the domestic space and destroy the son. In the last act of the film, the mother herself embodies these destructive forces and attempts to strangle the child. Before his mother can kill him, the boy caresses her face and looks into her eyes, at which point the mother relents, and a black fluid projects from her mouth: a kind of purification has taken place. It is then that the mother can reclaim a protective maternal position. She stands up, faces the monster, and forces it away from her son. But the story (which until now follows a traditional narrative trajectory) does not end here. In a conclusion consistent with Parker's (1995) proposals on the need for mothers to integrate their contradictory feelings towards their children, the monster is 'invited' to stay with them in the basement of the house. In the final scene, mother and son prepare food for it. The monster is separated but, at the same time, connected to the rest of the house. Could these operations serve as a model for trauma work in therapy?

Having achieved a higher level of reflexivity, explicit, and controlled work with the film material (partially related to Wolz's 2010 prescriptive way [2010]) can help the patient re-own those affective elements that have been defensively dissociated. This work is based on the premise that monstrous imagery can be seen as "an initial, symbolic emergence of traumatic experience into awareness [which] may present an opportunity to face, process and piece together fragmented traumatic experience; a function of an adaptive self-actualizing drive towards growth and psychological homeostasis" (Hamilton, 2020, p.2).

While some of the previously described strategies anticipate this therapeutic goal, what we propose here is a more systematized approach to personal exploration of horror cinema metaphors. Wolz, for example, describes a possible conversational sequence that starts by observing characters (or monsters, from our horror cinema-focused perspective) that the client reacts to with dislike, follows with the examination of whether what appears on the screen "might be part of your not-yet-fully-recognized positive qualities or repressed shadow self" (p. 205), and culminates by embracing and integrating these negative aspects as a condition of emotional healing (Wolz, 2010). With the help of a psychotherapist who always works within the patient's window of tolerance, this would be equivalent to transforming an "alien" aspect of the self that never underwent the process of mentalization (Fonagy et al., 2003) into articulated, understandable, and to some extent, communicable material.

Putting the characters on the couch

In a final therapeutic movement, fully related to Wolz's prescriptive way (2010), the therapeutic conversation could revolve around a more "practical" use of the film metaphor, by asking questions such as: "What does this character do to confront the monsters that harms them?" "What could they do differently?" "In what ways do their strategies to escape make them vulnerable to new visits from the ghost or new attacks from the post-traumatic monster?"

More specifically, patient and therapist can: 1. embark on an analysis of the motivations, fears, and defenses of the film's characters; 2. explore alternative coping paths and creative or adaptive ways in which the character could face the dangers represented in the film (both internal and external); 3. engage in the collaborative creation of stories similar to the one told in the film, but better suited to the patient's conflict or to endings that would be healthier.

Many characters in traumatic horror lend themselves to a psychoanalytic reading of their motivations, conflicts, and defenses. Consider again *Gerald's Game* (Flanagan, 2017). The film's main character is a woman who, while a child, was molested by her father. Now, after her husband dies during an aggressive sexual game, she must confront her inner demons and escape her handcuffs while battling hallucinations and memories. Without her being aware, the sexual intercourse game with her husband is a reenactment of the helplessness and fear experienced when her father abused her. A patient who thinks about the reasons why Gerald's wife submits to her husband and allows herself to be tied to the bed is, indirectly, talking about how their own past influences their experience of themselves and their ways of relating in the realm of intimacy, how inadvertently their interpersonal patterns lead to re-victimization, or how the very tools they use to avoid being hurt again paradoxically isolate or expose them to new instances of trauma.

Putting the characters of horror cinema on the couch can help patients and therapists uncover the psychodynamics of the characters, which would serve on a psychoeducational level (as a way to understand traumatic processes) but also promote insight (as a way to "see oneself" by looking at others).

Coda

In line with what has been raised in this chapter, we could imagine one last way in which horror fiction can be beneficial from a therapeutic point of view, and that is its ultimate message: you cannot escape forever, the only way to free yourself from the monster is to turn around and stand up to it. The key is, therefore, to regain agency and *do something*, to abandon the state of perpetual flight and adopt a new behavior: even when the characters in horror movies make wrong decisions and die in the jaws of the monster, they are confirming that fundamental aspect of the narrative: what you do *matters*, your destiny is not indifferent to your actions. The 'final girl' survives because she has been courageous enough to look directly at the object of her terror and has taken action (often a ritual, symbolic kind); that is, she has taken responsibility for the outcome of her story. In other words, horror fiction dramatically – and physically – vindicates the importance of regaining agency and personal initiative precisely at the moments when we are most vulnerable and trapped by our fears.

References

Abramenko, E. (Director). (2020). *Sputnik* [Film]. Art Pictures Studio, Fond Kino.
Aja, A. (Director). (2008). *Mirrors* [Film]. Regency Enterprises.
Aldrich, R. (Director). (1962). *What Ever Happened to Baby Jane?* [Film]. Seven Arts Productions.
Alfredson, T. (Director). (2008). *Låt den rätte komma in* [Film]. EFTI.
Almodóvar, P. (Director). (2011). *The Skin I Live In* [Film]. El Deseo.
Amenábar, A. (Director). (2001). *The Others* [Film]. Las Producciones del Escorpión.
Anderson, J. (Director) (2008). *Lake Mungo* [Film]. Mungo Productions.
Anvari, B. (Director). (2016). *Under the Shadow* [Film]. Wigwam Film.
APPIVideo. (2018, April 30). Video 4. Identifying the Dominant Object Relations. *Caligor/APA Publishing* [Video]. YouTube. https://www.youtube.com/watch?v=oidaZgx493c.
Arnold, S. (2016). *Maternal Horror Film: Melodrama and Motherhood*. Springer.
Aronofsky, D. (Director). (2010). *Black Swan* [Film]. Cross Creek Pictures.
Aster, A. (Director). (2018). *Hereditary* [Film]. A24.
Aster, A. (Director). (2019). *Midsommar* [Film]. A24
Aster, A. (2017). *Midsommar* [Script]. A24
Atwood, G. & Stolorow, R. (2014). *Structures of Subjectivity: Explorations in Psychoanalytic Phenomenology and Contextualism*. Routledge.
Aznar Alarcón, F.J. & Varela Feal, N. (October, 2019). La restauración de la competencia narrativa en el trauma relacional. Análisis de un caso. *Aperturas Psicoanalíticas* (62). Retrieved from https://www.aperturas.org/imagenes/archivos/ap2019%7Dn062a11.pdf.
Badley, L. (1996). *Writing Horror and the Body: The Fiction of Stephen King, Clive Barker, and Anne Rice: 51 (Contributions to the Study of Popular Culture)*, p. 75.
Barker, C. (1985). The Forbidden. *Books of Blood: Volume 5*. Sphere.
Barkham, M., Margison, F., Hardy, G.E., & Guthrie, E. (2016). *Psychodynamic-interpersonal Therapy: A Conversational Model*. Sage Publications.
Bartlett, F.C. (1932). *Remembering: A Study in Experimental and Social Psychology*. Cambridge University Press.
Bartlett, J.D., Kotake, C., Fauth, R., & Easterbrooks, M.A. (2017). Intergenerational transmission of child abuse and neglect: Do maltreatment type, perpetrator, and substantiation status matter? *Child Abuse & Neglect*, 63, 84–94. doi:10.1016/j.chiabu.2016.11.021.
Beebe, B., & Lachmann, F. M. (2014). *The Origins of Attachment*. Routledge.
Benau, K. (2022). *Shame, Pride, and Relational Trauma: Concepts and Psychotherapy*. Routledge.
Benjamin, J. (2017). *Beyond Doer and Done To: Recognition Theory, Intersubjectivity and the Third*. Routledge.
Benyakar, M. & Lezica, A. (2005). *Lo traumático: Clínica & paradoja*. Biblos.
Bion, W.R. (1962). *Learning From Experience*. Heinemann.

Boulanger, G. (2011). *Wounded by Reality: Understanding and Treating Adult Onset Trauma*. Taylor & Francis.
Bowlby, J. (1980). *Attachment and Loss. Vol. 3: Loss: Sadness and Depression*. Basic Books.
Breuer, J., & Freud, S. (1895). *Studies on Hysteria*. Basic Books.
Brewin, C.R., Dalgleish, T., & Joseph, S. (1996). A dual representation theory of posttraumatic stress disorder. *Psychological Review*, 103(4), 670–686.
Briere, J. (2006). *Principles of Trauma Therapy: A Guide to Symptoms, Evaluation, and Treatment*. Sage Publications.
Bromberg, P.M. (2009). *Awakening the Dreamer: Clinical Journeys*. Routledge.
Bromberg, P.M. (2011). *The Shadow of the Tsunami: and the Growth of the Relational Mind*. Routledge.
Bromberg, P.M. (1998). *Standing in the Spaces: Essays on Clinical Process, Trauma, and Dissociation*. Analytic Press.
Bruckner, D. (Director). (2021). *The Night House* [Film]. Searchlight Pictures.
Caligor, E., Kernberg, O.F., Clarkin, J.F., & Yeomans, F.E. (2018). *Psychodynamic Therapy for Personality Pathology: Treating Self and Interpersonal Functioning*. American Psychiatric Pub.
Campbell, J. (1949). *The Hero with a Thousand Faces*. Princeton University Press.
Campbell, J. (1938). Who goes there? *Astounding Science Fiction*, 21(2), 60–97.
Carpenter, J. (Director). (1980). *The Fog* [Film]. AVCO Embassy Pictures, Debra Hill.
Carpenter, J. (Director). (1978). *Halloween* [Film]. Compass International Pictures, Falcon International Productions
Carpenter, J. (Director). (1982). *The Thing* [Film]. Universal Pictures.
Carroll, N. (1990). *The Philosophy of Horror, or Paradoxes of the Heart*. Routledge
Caruth, C. (2013). Traumatic awakenings. In Parker, A. & Sedgwick, E.K. (Eds.), *Performativity and Performance*. Routledge. [Original work published 1996.]
Chaganty, A. (Director) (2020). *Run*. Summit Entertainment.
Chong, C.Y.J. (2015). Why art psychotherapy? Through the lens of interpersonal neurobiology: The distinctive role of art psychotherapy intervention for clients with early relational trauma. *International Journal of Art Therapy*, 20(3), 118–126.
Clark, A. (2013). Whatever next? Predictive brains, situated agents, and the future of cognitive science. *Behavioral and Brain Sciences*, 36(3), 181–204.
Clark, B. (Director). (1974). *Deathdream* [Film]. Impact Films, Quadrant Films.
Clasen, M. (2017). *Why Horror Seduces*. Oxford University Press.
Clover, C.J. (2015). *Men, Women, and Chain Saws: Gender in the Modern Horror Film – Updated Edition*. Vol. 15. Princeton University Press.
Clute, J. (2006). *The Darkening Garden: A Short Lexicon of Horror*. Payseur & Schmidt.
Coppola, F.F. (Director) (1992). *Bram Stoker's Dracula* [Film]. Columbia Pictures, American Zoetrope.
Courtois, C.A., & Ford, J.D. (2009). *Treating Complex Traumatic Stress Disorders: An Evidence-based Guide*. Guilford Press.
Crastnopol, M. (2015). *Micro-trauma: A Psychoanalytic Understanding of Cumulative Psychic Injury*. Routledge.
Craven, W. (Director). (1984). *A Nightmare on Elm Street* [Film]. New Line Cinema.
Craven, W. (Director). (1972). *Last House on the Left* [Film]. Lobster Enterprises, Sean S. Cunningham.
Craven, W. (Director). (1996). *Scream* [Film]. Dimension Films, Woods Entertainment.
Cregger, Z. (Director). (2022). *Barbarian* [Film]. Boulderlight Pictures, Hammerstone Studios.
Critchfield, K.L. & Benjamin, L.S. (2008). Internalized representations of early interpersonal experience and adult relationships: A test of copy process theory in clinical and non–clinical settings. *Psychiatry: Interpersonal and Biological Processes*, 71(1), 71–92.

Crittenden, P.M. (2016). *Raising Parents: Attachment, Representation, and Treatment* (2nd ed.). Routledge.
Cronenberg, D. (Director). (1979). *The Brood* [Film]. CFDC, Elgin International Films.
Cronenberg, D. (Director). (1983). *The Dead Zone* [Film]. Dino de Laurentiis, Lorimar.
Cronenberg, D. (Director). (1986). *The Fly* [Film]. Brooksfilms, SLM Production.
Cronenberg, D. (Director). (2002). *Spider* [Film]. Sony Pictures, Capitol Films.
Crump, A. (2020). The new wave of horror movies suggest we should embrace our terrifying reality. *Polygon*. Retrieved from: https://www.polygon.com/2020/7/6/21314791/new-horror-movies-2020-relic-sea-fever.
Cunningham, S. (Director). (1980). *Friday the 13th* [Film]. Paramount Pictures.
DaCosta, N. (Director). (2021). *Candyman* [Film]. MGM, Monkeypaw Productions.
Davies, J.M. & Frawley, M.G. (1994). *Treating the Adult Survivor of Childhood Sexual Abuse: A Psychoanalytic Perspective*. Basic Books.
de Palma, B. (Director). (1976). *Carrie* [Film]. United Artists.
de Van, M. (Director). (2002). *Dans ma peau* [Film]. Lezennec & Associes, Canal+.
del Toro, G. (Director). (2001). *El espinazo del diablo* [Film]. El Deseo S.A.
Dell, P.F., & O'Neil, J.A. (Eds.). (2009). *Dissociation and the Dissociative Disorders: DSM-V and Beyond*. Routledge.
Demme, J. (Director). (1991). *The Silence of the Lambs* [Film]. Orion Pictures.
Dent, V. (2020). When the body keeps the score: Some implications of trauma theory and practice for psychoanalytic work. *Psychoanalytic Inquiry*, 40(6), 435–447.
Derrickson, S. (Director). (2012). *Sinister* [Film]. Blumhouse Productions.
Derry, C. (2009). *Dark Dreams 2.0: A Psychological History of the Modern Horror Film from the 1950s to the 21st Century*. McFarland.
Doka, K.J. (2017). Disenfranchised grief and trauma. In Thompson, N., Cox, G., & Stevenson, R.G. (Eds.). (2017). *Handbook of Traumatic Loss*. Routledge
Donaldson, R. (Director). (1995). *Species* [Film]. Metro-Goldwyn-Mayer.
du Maurier, D. (1971). Don't look now. *Don't look now and other stories*. Gollancz.
Eagle, M. (2018). *Core Concepts in Classical Psychoanalysis: Clinical, Research Evidence and Conceptual Critiques*. Routledge.
Eggers, R. (Director). (2015). *The Witch* [Film]. A24.
Ehlers, A. & Clark, D. M. (2000). A cognitive model of posttraumatic stress disorder. *Behaviour Research and Therapy*, 38(4), 319–345.
Eliade, M. (1964). *Shamanism: Archaic Techniques of Ecstasy*. Princeton University Press.
Eliade, M. (1976). *El chamanismo y las técnicas arcaicas del éxtasis*. Fondo de Cultura Económica.
Erreich, A. (2017). Unconscious fantasy and the priming phenomenon. *Journal of the American Psychoanalytic Association*, 65(2), 195–219.
Fairbairn, W.R.D. (1952a). *An Object Relations Theory of the Personality*. Basic Books.
Fairbairn, W.R.D. (1952b). *Psychoanalytic Studies of the Personality*. Routledge.
Ferenczi, S. (1933). Confusion of tongues between adults and the child. *International Journal of Psycho-Analysis*, 30, 225–230.
Fincher, D. (Director). (1999). *Fight Club* [Film]. 20th Century Fox.
Finn, P. (Director). (2022). *Smile* [Film]. Temple Hill Entertainment, Paramount Players.
Fisher, M. (2016). *The Weird and the Eerie*. Repeater Books.
Flanagan, M. (Director). (2017). *Gerald's Game* [Film]. Intrepid Pictures.
Flanagan, M. (Director). (2013). *Oculus* [Film]. Intrepid Pictures.
Fonagy, P., Gergely, G., Jurist, E.L., & Target, M. (2002). *Affect Regulation, Mentalization, and the Development of the Self*. Other Press.
Fonagy, P., Gergely, G., & Jurist, E.L. (2018). *Affect Regulation, Mentalization and the Development of the Self*. Routledge.

Fonagy, P., Luyten, P., & Allison, E. (2019). The dynamic self in psychodynamic practice: Interpersonal and intrapsychic dimensions. *Journal of the American Psychoanalytic Association, 67*(3), 507–532.

Fonagy, P., Target, M., Gergely, G., Allen, J.G., & Bateman, A.W. (2003). The developmental roots of borderline personality disorder in early attachment relationships: A theory and some evidence. *Psychoanalytic Inquiry, 23*(3), 412–459.

Fosha, D., Thoma, N., & Yeung, D. (2019). Transforming emotional suffering into flourishing: Metatherapeutic processing of positive affect as a trans-theoretical vehicle for change. *Counselling Psychology Quarterly, 32*(3–4), 563–593.

Foucault, M. (2008). Of other spaces. In Dehaene, M. & De Cauter, L., *Heterotopia in a Postcivil Society*, pp. 25–42. Routledge. [Original work published in 1967].

Fraiberg, S., Adelson, E., & Shapiro, V. (1975). Ghosts in the nursery. *Journal of American Academy of Child Psychiatry, 14*, 387–421.

Franju, G. (Director). (1960). *Les yeux sans visage* [Film]. Lux Film.

Frankel, J. (2002). Exploring Ferenczi's concept of identification with the aggressor: Its role in trauma, everyday life, and the therapeutic relationship. *Psychoanalytic Dialogues, 12*(1), 101–139.

Franz, V. & Fiala, S. (Directors). (2014). *Goodnight Mommy* [Film]. Ulrich Seidl Film Produktion GmbH.

Freud, A. (1936). *The Ego and the Mechanisms of Defence* (C. Baines, Trans.). Karnac Books.

Freud, S. (1961). *Beyond the pleasure principle* (J. Strachey, Trans.). W.W. Norton & Company. [Original work published in 1920.]

Freud, S. (1945). Mourning and melancholia. In J. Strachey (Ed. & Trans.), *The Standard Edition of the Complete Psychological Works of Sigmund Freud*, Vol. 14, pp. 237–258. Hogarth Press. [Original work published in 1917.]

Freud, S. (1945). The uncanny. In J. Strachey (Ed. & Trans.), *The Standard Edition of the Complete Psychological Works of Sigmund Freud*, Vol. 17, pp. 217–256. Hogarth Press. [Original work published in 1919.]

Fricker, M. (2007). *Epistemic Injustice: Power and the Ethics of Knowing*. OUP Oxford.

Friedkin, W. (Director). (1973). *The Exorcist* [Film]. Warner Bros.

Friston, K. (2010). The free-energy principle: A unified brain theory? *Nature Reviews Neuroscience, 11*(2), 127–138.

Gabbard, G.O. (2014). *Psychodynamic Psychiatry in Clinical Practice*. American Psychiatric Pub.

Garland, A. (Director). (2018). *Annihilation* [Film]. DNA Films, Paramount Pictures.

Glass, R. (Director). (2019). *Saint Maud* [Film]. Escape Plan Productions, BFI Film Fund.

Glazer, J. (Director) (2013). *Under the Skin* [Film]. Film4 Productions, Nick Wechsler Productions.

Gleiser, K.A. (2003). Psychoanalytic perspectives on traumatic repetition. *Journal of Trauma & Dissociation, 4*(2), 27–47.

Goddard, D. (Director). (2012). *The Cabin in the Woods* [Film]. Mutant Enemy Productions.

Hall, C. (2014). Bereavement theory: Recent developments in our understanding of grief and bereavement. *Bereavement Care, 33*(1), 6–12.

Hamilton, J. (2020). Monsters and posttraumatic stress: An experiential-processing model of monster imagery in psychological therapy, film and television. *Humanities and Social Sciences Communications, 7*(1), 1–8. https://doi.org/10.1057/s41599-020-00628-2.

Hamilton, J. & Sullivan, J. (2015). *Horror in Therapy: Working Creatively with Horror and Science Fiction Films in Trauma Therapy*. Amazon.

Hamm, N. (Director). (2004). *Godsend* [Film]. Lionsgate, 2929 Productions.

Han, B.-C. (2015). *The Transparency Society*. Stanford University Press.

Hanscomb, S. (2010). Existentialism and art-horror. *Sartre Studies International, 16*(1), 1–23.

Herman, J.L. (2015). *Trauma and Recovery: The Aftermath of Violence—From Domestic Abuse to Political Terror.* Hachette.
Hill, D. (2015). *Affect Regulation Theory: A Clinical Model (Norton Series on Interpersonal Neurobiology).* W.W. Norton & Company.
Hitchcock, A. (Director). (1963). *The Birds* [Film]. Universal Pictures.
Hitchcock, A. (Director). (1960). *Psycho* [Film]. Paramount Pictures.
Hofstadter, D.R., & Sander, E. (2013). *Surfaces and Essences: Analogy as the Fuel and Fire of Thinking.* Basic books.
Hohwy, J. (2013). *The Predictive Mind.* Oxford University Press.
Holland-Toll, L. J. (2001). *As American as Mom, Baseball, and Apple Pie: Constructing Community in Contemporary American Horror Fiction.* Popular Press.
Hooper, T. (Director). (1982). *Poltergeist* [Film]. MGM.
Hooper, T. (Director). (1974). *The Texas Chainsaw Massacre* [Film]. Bryanstone Pictures.
Ito, J. (1998). *Uzumaki.* Big Comic Spirits.
Jackson, S. (1959). *The Haunting of Hill House.* Viking.
Jackson, S. (1948). The Lottery. *The New Yorker.* Retrieved from: https://www.newyorker.com/magazine/1948/06/26/the-lottery.
James, N.E. (Director) (2020). *Relic* [Film]. AGBO, Carver Films, Film Victoria, Nine Stories Productions, Screen Australia.
Janet, P. (1907). *The Major Symptoms of Hysteria: Fifteen Lectures Given in the Medical School of Harvard University.* Macmillan.
Janoff-Bulman, R. (1992). *Shattered Assumptions: Towards a New Psychology of Trauma.* Free Press.
Johnstone, L. & Boyle, M. (Eds.). (2018). *The Power Threat Meaning Framework: Towards the Identification of Patterns in Emotional Distress, Unusual Experiences and Troubled or Troubling Behaviour, as an Alternative to Functional Psychiatric Diagnosis.* British Psychological Society.
Karpman, S. (1968). Fairy tales and script drama analysis. *Transactional Analysis Bulletin,* 7(26), 39–43.
Kaufman, P. (Director). (1978). *Invasion of the Body Snatchers* [Film]. Solofilm.
Kent, J. (Director). (2014). *The Babadook* [Film]. Causeway Films.
King, S. (1981). *Danse Macabre.* Everest House.
King, S. (1989). *The Dark Half.* Viking.
King, S. (1992). *Gerald's Game.* Viking.
King, S. (1977). *The Shining.* Doubleday.
King, S. (1978). *The Stand.* Doubleday.
King, S. (1978). They always come back. In *Night Shift.* Doubleday.
Kluft R.P. (2017). Weaponized sex: Defensive pseudo-erotic aggression in the service of safety. *Journal of Trauma & Dissociation,* 18(3), 259–283. https://doi.org/10.1080/15299732.2017.1295376.
Knafo, D. (2020). Film, psychotherapy, and the taming of rage at the mother. *Journal of Clinical Psychology,* 76(8), 1514–1519.
Koren-Karie, N., Oppenheim, D., & Getzler-Yosef, R. (2008). Shaping children's internal working models through mother–child dialogues: The importance of resolving past maternal trauma. *Attachment & Human Development,* 10(4), 465–483. https://doi.org/10.1080/14616730802461482.
Kosh, K. & Widmyer, D. (Director). (2019). *Pet Sematary* [Film]. Alphaville Films, Paramount Pictures.
Kube, T., Berg, M., Kleim, B., & Herzog, P. (2020). Rethinking post-traumatic stress disorder–A predictive processing perspective. *Neuroscience & Biobehavioral Reviews,* 113, 448–460.
Kubrick, S. (Director). (1980). *The Shining* [Film]. Hawk Films, Peregrine, Warner Bros.

References

Lalor, K., & McElvaney, R. (2010). Child sexual abuse, links to later sexual exploitation/high-risk sexual behavior, and prevention/treatment programs. *Trauma, Violence, & Abuse*, 11(4), 159–177.
Lambert, M. (Director). (1989). *Pet Sematary* [Film]. Paramount Pictures.
Lanius, R.A., Vermetten, E., & Pain, C. (Eds.). (2010). *The Impact of Early Life Trauma on Health and Disease: The Hidden Epidemic*. Cambridge University Press.
Lanius, R.A., Williamson, P.C., Densmore, M., Boksman, K., Gupta, M.A., Neufeld, R.W., … & Menon, R.S. (2004). The nature of traumatic memories: A 4-T FMRI functional connectivity analysis. *American Journal of Psychiatry*, 161(1), 36–44.
Laub, D. (2005). Traumatic shutdown of narrative and symbolization: A death instinct derivative? *Contemporary Psychoanalysis*, 41(2), 307–326. https://doi.org/10.1080/00107530.2005.10745863.
Levine, P.A. (2010). *In an Unspoken Voice: How the Body Releases Trauma and Restores Goodness*. North Atlantic Books.
Lévi-Strauss, C. (1966). *The Savage Mind*. University of Chicago Press.
Lévi-Strauss, C. (1987). *Antropología Estructural*. Ediciones Paidós.
Liotti, G. (2004). Trauma, dissociation, and disorganized attachment: Three strands of a single braid. *Psychotherapy: Theory, Research, Practice, Training*, 41(4), 472.
Liotti, G. (2011). Attachment disorganization and the clinical dialogue: Theme and variations. In Solomon, J. & George, C. (2011). *Disorganized Attachment and Caregiving*, pp. 383–413. Guilford Press.
Lovecraft, H.P. (1927). The colour out of space. *Amazing Stories*, 2(6), 557–567.
Lowenstein, A. (2005). *Shocking Representation: Historical Trauma, National Cinema, and the Modern Horror Film*. Columbia University Press.
Lynch, D. (Director). (1986). *Blue Velvet* [Film]. De Laurentiis Entertainment Group.
Lynch, D. (Director). (1990). *Twin Peaks* [Series]. Lynch/Frost Productions, Propaganda Films.
Lyons-Ruth, K., Bronfman, E., & Parsons, E. (1999). Atypical maternal behavior and disorganized infant attachment strategies: Frightened, frightening, and atypical maternal behavior and disorganized infant attachment strategies. *Monographs of the Society for Research in Child Development*, 64(3), 67–96.
Lyons-Ruth, K., Bruschweiler-Stern, N., Harrison, A.M., Morgan, A.C., Nahum, J.P., Sander, L., … & Tronick, E.Z. (1998). Implicit relational knowing: Its role in development and psychoanalytic treatment. *Infant Mental Health Journal*, 19(3), 282–289.
Lyons-Ruth, K. & Jacobvitz, D. (2016). Attachment disorganization from infancy to adulthood: Neurobiological correlates, parenting contexts, and pathways to disorder. In Cassidy, J. & Shaver, P.R. (Eds.). *Handbook of Attachment: Theory, Research, and Clinical Applications*, pp. 667–695. Guilford Press.
MacLean, P.D. (1990). *The Triune Brain in Evolution: Role in Paleocerebral Functions*. Springer.
Main, M., & Solomon, J. (1990). Procedures for identifying infants as disorganized/disoriented during the Ainsworth Strange Situation. In Greenberg, M.T., Cicchetti, D., & Cummings, E.M. (Eds.), *Attachment in the Preschool Years: Theory, Research, and Intervention*, pp. 121–160. University of Chicago Press.
Martínez-Biurrun, I. & Pitillas, C. (2021). *Soy lo que me persigue: El terror como ficción del trauma*. Dilatando Mentes.
McDougall, J. (1989). *Theaters of the Body: A Psychoanalytic Approach to Psychosomatic Illness*. W.W. Norton & Company.
McEwen, B.S. (2007). Physiology and neurobiology of stress and adaptation: Central role of the brain. *Physiological Reviews*, 87(3), 873–904.
Meaney, M.J. & Szyf, M. (2005). Environmental programming of stress responses through DNA methylation: Life at the interface between a dynamic environment and a fixed genome. *Dialogues in Clinical Neuroscience*, 7(2), 103–123.

Medak, P. (Director). (1980). *The Changeling* [Film]. Chessman Park Productions.
Meins, E., Fernyhough, C., Wainwright, R., Gupta, M.D., Fradley, E., & Tuckey, M. (2002). Maternal mind-mindedness and attachment security as predictors of theory of mind understanding. *Child Development*, *73*(6), 1715–1726. https://doi.org/10.1111/1467-8624.00501.
Mihalka, G. (Director). (1981). *My Bloody Valentine* [Film]. Canadian Film Development Corporation, Secret Film Company.
Mitchell, D.R. (Director). (2014). *It Follows* [Film]. Northern Lights Films.
Modell, A.H. (2005). Emotional memory, metaphor, and meaning. *Psychoanalytic Inquiry*, *25*(4), 555–568.
Modell, A.H. (2009). Metaphor—The bridge between feelings and knowledge. *Psychoanalytic Inquiry*, *29*(1), 6–11.
Modell, A.H. (1997). The synergy of memory, affects and metaphor. *Journal of Analytical Psychology*, *42*(1), 105–117.
Monk, A. (2023). *Trauma and the Supernatural in Psychotherapy: Working with the Curse Position in Clinical Practice*. Taylor & Francis.
Muschietti, A. (Director). (2017). *It* [Film]. New Line Cinema, KatzSmith Productions.
Nakata, H. (Director). (2002). *Dark Water* [Film]. Oz Company, Kadokawa Shoten.
Nyby, C. (Director). (1951). *The Thing from Another World* [Film]. RKO Radio Pictures.
O'Bannon, D. & Lohr, M.R. (2013). *Dan O'Bannon's Guide to Screenplay Structure: Inside Tips from the Writer of Alien, Total Recall and Return of the Living Dead*. Michael Wiese Productions.
Ogden, P., Minton, K., & Pain, C. (2006). *Trauma and the Body: A Sensorimotor Approach to Psychotherapy*. W. W. Norton & Company.
Ong, A.D., Fuller-Rowell, T.E., & Bonanno, G.A. (2018). Prospective patterns of resilience and maladjustment during widowhood. *Psychology and Aging*, *19*(2), 260–271.
Oppenheim, D., & Koren-Karie, N. (2021). Parental insightfulness and parent–child emotion dialogues: Shaping children's internal working models. In Thompson, R.A., Simpson, J. A., & Berlin, L. J. (Eds.), *Attachment: The Fundamental Questions*, pp. 248–263. Guilford Publications.
Parker, R. (1995). *Mother Love/Mother Hate: The Power of Maternal Ambivalence*. Basic Books.
Peak, D. (2014). *The Spectacle of the Void*. Schism Press.
Peele, J. (Director). (2022). *Nope.* [Film]. Universal Pictures, Monkeypaw Productions.
Peele, J. (Director). (2019). *Us.* [Film]. Monkeypaw Productions, Perfect World Pictures.
Peli, O. (Director). (2007). *Paranormal Activity* [Film]. Blumhouse Productions.
Pérez, J.D. (2018). Hacia una (re) vocalización del trauma: una crítica a Caruth desde la ética de la escucha. *Perífrasis. Revista de Literatura, Teoría & Crítica*, *9*(18), 117–133.
Perl, O., Duek, O., Kulkarni, K.R., Gordon, C., Krystal, J.H., Levy, I., … & Schiller, D. (2023). Neural patterns differentiate traumatic from sad autobiographical memories in PTSD. *Nature Neuroscience*, *26*(12), 2226–2236.
Perry, B.D., Pollard, R.A., Blakley, T.L., Baker, W.L., & Vigilante, D. (1995). Childhood trauma, the neurobiology of adaptation, and "use-dependent" development of the brain: How "states" become "traits". *Infant Mental Health Journal*, *16*(4), 271–291.
Philipou, D. & Philipou, M. (Director). (2022). *Talk to Me* [Film]. Causeway Films.
Pitillas, C. (2020). Las dinámicas interpersonales del trauma a lo largo del desarrollo: supervivencia, transformaciones, repetición. In Meana, R. & Martínez, C. (Eds.), *Abuso y sociedad contemporánea: reflexiones multidisciplinares*. Thompson Reuters Aranzadi.
Pitts, B.L., Eisenberg, M.L., Bailey, H.R., & Zacks, J.M. (2022). PTSD is associated with impaired event processing and memory for everyday events. *Cognitive Research: Principles and Implications*, *7*(1), 35.
Polanski, R. (Director). (1965). *Repulsion* [Film]. Compton Films.

Quammen, D. (2003). *Monster of God: The Man-eating Predator in the Jungles of History and the Mind*. W.W. Norton & Company.
Raimi, S. (Director). (1981). *The Evil Dead* [Film]. Renaissance Pictures.
Ratner, B. (Director). (2002). *Red Dragon* [Film]. Universal Pictures, De Laurentiis.
Rauch, S.L., Shin, L.M., & Phelps, E.A. (2006). Neurocircuitry models of posttraumatic stress disorder and extinction: human neuroimaging research—past, present, and future. *Biological Psychiatry*, 60(4), 376–382.
Reiner, R. (Director). (1990). *Misery* [Film]. Castle Rock Entertainment.
Richman, S. (2006). Finding one's voice: Transforming trauma into autobiographical narrative. *Contemporary Psychoanalysis*, 42(4), 639–650.
Roas, D. (2016). *Tras los límites de lo real: una definición de lo fantástico*. Editorial Páginas de Espuma.
Roeg, N. (Director). (1973). *Don't Look Now* [Film]. Paramount Pictures.
Romero, G.A. (Director). (1993). *The Dark Half* [Film]. Orion Pictures.
Romero, G.A. (Director). (1968). *Night of the Living Dead* [Film]. Image Ten.
Rose, B. (Director). (1992). *Candyman* [Film]. Propaganda Films, Candyman Films.
Salva, V. (Director). (2001). *Jeepers Creepers* [Film]. Cinerenta Cinebeta, American Zoetrope.
Saramago, J. (2002). *O Homem Duplicado*. Caminho.
Schore, A.N. (2021). The interpersonal neurobiology of intersubjectivity. *Frontiers in Psychology*, 1366. doi: 10.3389/fpsyg.2021.648616.
Schwartz, H. (2000). *Dialogues With Forgotten Voices: Relational Perspectives On Child Abuse Trauma And The Treatment Of Severe Dissociative Disorders*. Hachette.
Scott, J.C., Matt, G.E., Wrocklage, K.M., Crnich, C., Jordan, J., Southwick, S.M., Krystal, J.H., & Schweinsburg, B.C. (2015). A quantitative meta-analysis of neurocognitive functioning in posttraumatic stress disorder. *Psychological Bulletin*, 141(1), 105–140. https://doi.org/10.1037/a0038039.
Scott, R. (Director). (1979). *Alien* [Film]. Brandywine Productions.
Shymalan, M.N. (Director). (2002). Signs. Touchstone Pictures.
Shyamalan, M.N. (Director). (1999). *The Sixth Sense* [Film]. Buena Vista Pictures.
Shyamalan, M.N. (Director). (2016). *Split* [Film]. Blinding Edge Pictures, Blumhouse Productions.
Shyamalan, M.N. (Director). (2004). *The Village* [Film]. Touchstone Pictures, Blinding Edge Pictures.
Sinason, V. (Ed.). (2002). *Attachment, Trauma and Multiplicity: Working With Dissociative Identity Disorder*. Psychology Press.
Slade, A. (2005). Parental reflective functioning: An introduction. *Attachment & Human Development*, 7(3), 269–281.
Slade, A. & Cohen, L.J. (1996). The process of parenting and the remembrance of things past. *Infant Mental Health Journal: Official Publication of The World Association for Infant Mental Health*, 17(3), 217–238.
Sluzky, C. (2006). Victimización, recuperación y las historias "con mejor forma". *Revista Sistemas familiares y otros sistemas humanos*, 22(1–2), 5–20.
Solomon, J., & George, C. (Eds.). (2011). *Disorganized Attachment and Caregiving*. Guilford Press.
Spielberg, S. (Director). (1975). *Jaws* [Film]. Zanuck/Brown.
Stanley, R. (Director). (2019). *Color Out of Space* [Film]. Spectre Vision, ACE Pictures Entertainment, XYZ Films.
Stein, D.J., Koenen, K.C., Friedman, M.J., & Hill, E.D. (Eds.). (2013). *Post-Traumatic Stress Disorder*. Wiley-Blackwell.
Stern, D. (1985). *The Interpersonal World of the Infant: A View From Psychoanalysis and Developmental Psychology*. Routledge.

Stern, D.B. (2013). *Unformulated Experience: From Dissociation to Imagination in Psychoanalysis*. Routledge.
Stern, D.B. (2012). Witnessing across time: Accessing the present from the past and the past from the present. *The Psychoanalytic Quarterly*, 81(1), 53–81.
Stern, D.N. (2010). *Forms of Vitality: Exploring Dynamic Experience in Psychology, Arts, Psychotherapy, and Development*. Oxford University Press.
Stern, D.N. (2005). Intersubjectivity. In Gabbard, G.O., Litowitz, B.E., & Williams, P. (Eds.), *Textbook of Psychoanalysis*. American Psychiatric Publishing.
Stevenson, R.L. (1886). *The Strange Case of Dr. Jekyll and Mr. Hyde*. Longman's Green & Co.
Stolorow, R.D., & Atwood, G.E. (1992). *Contexts of Being: The Intersubjective Foundations of Psychological Life*. Routledge.
Terr, L. (1990). *Too Scared to Cry: Psychic Trauma in Childhood*. Basic Books.
Tisseron, S. (2007) Transmissions et ricochets de la vie psychique entre les générations. *La revue internationale de l'éducation familiale*, 22, 13–26. http://dx.doi.org/10.3917/rief.022.0013.
Thacker, E. (2011). *In the Dust of This Planet: Horror of Philosophy Vol. 1*. Zero Books.
Thomas, K. (Director). (2019). *The Vigil* [Film]. BoulderLight Pictures, Blumhouse Productions.
Thornberry, T.P., & Henry, K.L. (2013). Intergenerational continuity in maltreatment. *Journal of Abnormal Child Psychology*, 41, 555–569.
Turner, R.B. & Stauffer, S.D. (Eds.). (2023). *Disenfranchised Grief: Examining Social, Cultural, and Relational Impacts*. Taylor & Francis.
van der Kolk, B. (2015). *The Body Keeps the Score: Brain, Mind and Body in the Healing of Trauma*. Penguin Books.
van der Linden, M. & Schapiro, A.C. (2017). Sequential learning and the neural substrates of memory: Insights from the AG-hippocampus interplay. *Journal of Neuroscience*, 37(31), 7555–7565.
Vandermeer, J. (2014). *Annihilation*. Farrar, Straus and Giroux.
Verbinski, G. (Director). (2002). *The Ring* [Film]. DreamWorks SKG, BenderSpink.
Villaronga, A. (Director). (1986). *Tras el cristal* [Film]. TEM Productores.
Villeneuve, D. (Director). (2013). *Enemy* [Film]. Rombus Media, Roxbury Pictures, Mecanismo Films.
Volkan, V.D. (2018). *Psychoanalysis, International Relations, and Diplomacy: A Sourcebook on Large-group Psychology*. Routledge.
Wachtel, P.L. (2014). *Cyclical Psychodynamics and the Contextual Self: The Inner World, the Intimate World, and the World of Culture and Society*. Routledge/Taylor & Francis.
Wachtel, P.L. (1997). *Psychoanalysis, Behavior Therapy, and the Relational World*. American Psychological Association.
Wan, J. (Director). (2013). *The Conjuring* [Film]. Warner Bros, New Line Cinema.
Wan, J. (Director). (2010). *Insidious* [Film]. Haunted Movies, Stage 6 Films, Alliance Films, IM Global.
Wedding, D. & Niemiec, R.M. (2003). The clinical use of films in psychotherapy. *Journal of Clinical Psychology*, 59(2), 207–215.
Weekes, R. (Director). (2020). *His House* [Film]. Regency Interprises.
White, S. (Director). (2018). *Slender Man* [Film]. Mythology Entertainment, Madhouse Entertainment.
Wilde, O. (2008). *The Picture of Dorian Gray*. Oxford University Press. [Original work published 1890].
Winnicott, D.W. (1953). Transitional objects and transitional phenomena; A study of the first not-me possession. *International Journal of Psycho-Analysis*, 34, 89–97.
Wise, R. (Director). (1963). *The Haunting* [Film]. Metro-Goldwyn-Mayer.

Wolz, B. (2010). Cinema as alchemy for healing and transformation: Using the power of films in psychotherapy and coaching. In Gregerson, M.B. (Ed.). *The Cinematic Mirror for Psychology and Life Coaching*, pp. 201–225. Springer.

Wyndham, J. (1951). *The Day of the Triffids*. Michael Joseph.

Yehuda, R. (Host). (2023, December 8). How trauma travels through generations and changes your genes [Podcast]. *The Human Upgrade*. Retrieved from: https://podcasts.apple.com/kz/podcast/how-trauma-travels-through-generations-and-changes/id451295014?i=1000501758267.

Yehuda, R. & Lehrner, A. (2018). Intergenerational transmission of trauma effects: Putative role of epigenetic mechanisms. *World Psychiatry*, 17(3), 243–257.

Zulawski, A. (Director). (1981). *Possession* [Film]. Gaumont, Oliane Productions.

Index

A

abuse, 1–2, 12, 14, 23–24, 32, 43–44, 52–53, 57, 60–61, 66–67, 69, 70, 72–74, 77, 82, 84, 89, 108, 114, 116, 121
acceptance, 79–80, 82, 90, 96
Aja, Alexander, 43, 94, 116
Alien, 29, 79, 80, 95, 97, 101, 122–123
allegorical moment, 96, 111–112
allegory/metaphor/symbol, 4–5, 9, 18, 30, 31–32, 41, 59, 62, 64–65, 67, 80, 86, 89, 96, 98, 100, 107–108, 112
alternative language, 58–59
Amenábar, Alejandro, 4, 54, 89, 116
amygdala, 22, 28, 56–57, 78
Annihilation, 71, 84, 119, 124
Anvari, Babak, 94, 116
Aronofsky, Darren, 10
Aster, Ari, 1, 16, 22, 43, 75, 83, 86, 89, 92, 94, 102–104, 116
attachment, 8, 15, 40, 45, 47, 52–53, 63, 69, 119, 121–122
authority (failure of), 2, 9, 25, 62, 79–80, 87–89, 91, 112

B

Babadook, The, 4, 15–16, 26, 40, 55, 79–81, 83–84, 88–89, 93, 97, 100, 110, 113, 120
Barker, Clive, 19, 94, 116
basement, 11, 19, 30–32, 34, 65, 67, 73, 83–84, 87, 92, 100, 110, 112–113
basic assumptions, 4, 6, 8–10, 12, 14, 16–17, 47, 80, 82, 96, 105, 112
Black Swan, 10, 26, 41, 42, 116
Blue Velvet, 19, 121
body, 5, 9, 12–14, 22, 28–31, 34–35, 38, 45, 50–52, 54, 56–57, 64–65, 67–68, 72, 75, 91–93, 96, 98–100, 102, 105–106, 112, 118
body horror, 12
brain, 22, 27–28, 57, 124
Bram Stoker's Dracula, 38, 111, 117
Brood, The, 12–13, 118
Bruckner, David, 4, 83, 117

C

Candyman, 43, 94, 118, 123
Carpenter, John, 14, 17, 50–51, 82, 88, 98, 117
Carrie, 15, 26, 43, 92, 98, 100, 118
Changeling, The, 4, 30–31, 60, 83, 101, 122
children, 2–3, 15–16, 23, 25–26, 31, 52, 54, 61–64, 66, 69, 72–75, 77–78, 84, 86, 88–89, 94, 98, 113, 120, 122
Clark, Bob, 21, 34, 58, 64, 107, 117–118
Clute, John, 18–19, 54, 81–82, 112, 117
Color Out of Space, 16, 18, 77–78, 123
condensation, 81
conflict, 15, 34, 36, 38, 48, 51–52, 54, 66, 75–76, 81, 110, 111, 113–114
Conjuring, The, 4, 31, 124
contemporary horror, 3
conversion, 59, 90
cosmic horror, 18, 77
Craven, Wes, 13, 19, 31, 61, 87, 95–97, 100–101, 117
Cregger, Zack, 83–84, 117
Cronenberg, David, 12–13, 46, 59, 93, 100, 118
Cunningham, Sean, 82, 117–118
curse/haunt/haunting, 1–2, 4–5, 9, 20, 31–32, 70, 74, 80, 83, 86–87, 92–93, 102, 107
cyclicity, 82

D

Dark Half, The, 10, 120, 123
Dark Water, 16, 32, 76, 78, 122
David Lynch, 19
Day of the Triffids, 17, 125
De Palma, Brian, 15, 26, 43, 92, 98, 100, 118
Deathdream, 64, 117
defense, 4–5, 24, 29, 39–40, 108, 110, 113
Demme, Jonathan, 98, 118
denial, 6, 24, 38, 52, 77, 79–80, 85
Derrickson, Scott, 81, 118
Devil's Backbone, The, 4, 31
dis/ease, 18–19
disaffirmative, 101
disjointed time, 61
disorganization, 2, 5, 52–53, 63, 121
displacement, 4, 84, 87
dissociation, 4–6, 11–12, 15, 22–26, 29, 31–32, 39–43, 45, 53–54, 66–67, 70, 80, 83–86, 91, 99, 101, 106, 108, 111–114, 117, 118–121, 123–124
Don't Look Now, 36, 83, 111, 123
double/doppelgänger, 10–11, 19
dream, 5, 11, 52, 61–62, 66, 78, 84, 103, 106

E

eerie, the, 10, 17
Eggers, Robert, 104, 118
embracing the monster, 5, 110, 113
Enemy, 11, 119, 124
Exorcist, The, 54, 81, 85, 90, 97, 119

F

failure of language, 88
family trauma, 1–2, 8–9, 11, 13–16, 18–19, 22, 25–26, 30–35, 37, 39–42, 45–49, 53–55, 60–66, 72–78, 81–86, 88–90, 92, 94, 97–98, 100, 102–103, 110–113, 120, 122
Fight Club, 108
Finn, Parker, 83, 102, 104, 118
Flanagan, Mike, 67, 108, 118
Fog, The, 50–51, 117
fragmentation, 6, 11, 32–33, 35, 37, 39–45, 47, 49, 53, 112
free association, 66
freeze response, 21–26, 34, 37, 64, 66, 99, 106
Friedkin, William, 54, 81, 85, 90, 97, 100, 119

G

Garland, Alex, 71, 84, 119
Gerald's Game, 67, 68, 108, 114, 118, 120
ghost, 2, 4, 9, 43, 48–49, 54, 58, 60–61, 73–75, 77, 84, 93, 101, 107, 111, 114
Glass, Rose, 43, 59, 72, 119
Goodnight Mommy, 26
guilt, 37–38, 43, 51, 71, 81, 87, 93, 103

H

haunted house, 31–32
Haunting, The, 48–49, 83, 98, 120, 124
Haunting of Hill House, The, 48, 120
Hereditary, 1, 16, 75–76, 78, 83, 86, 89, 92, 94, 102, 116
heterotopia, 12, 83–84, 99
His House, 4, 54–55, 79–80, 83, 86, 93, 124
Hitchcock, Alfred, 11, 15, 17, 26, 30–31, 48, 65, 83, 87, 98, 104, 112, 120
Hooper, Tobe, 13, 43, 79–80, 87, 89–90, 97, 100–101, 104, 120
humiliation, 52–53, 72, 74, 98

I

identification with the aggressor, 12, 47, 74
identity, 6, 8, 10–11, 14, 18, 20, 23, 33–34, 39–41, 43–45, 47, 54, 62, 66
imprinting, 68
In a Glass Cage, 43, 72
In My Skin, 44
intergenerational trauma, 97
introject, 11–12, 29, 37, 38, 47, 49
intrusion, 52, 54, 57, 85
intrusive thoughts, 54, 72
Invasion of the Body Snatchers, 14, 120
It, 70, 82, 122
It Follows, 1, 3–4, 96, 122

J

Jaws, 87, 90, 95, 98, 123
Jeepers Creepers, 94, 123

K

Kent, Jennifer, 4, 15–16, 26, 40, 55, 79–80, 83–84, 88–89, 100–101, 113, 120
King, Stephen, 4, 10–11, 17, 26, 32, 36, 68, 78, 116
Kubrick, Stanley, 32, 43, 83, 94, 120

L

Last House on the Left, The, 13
Let the Right One In, 2
limbic system, 28, 55, 56
loss/grief, 4, 7, 15, 22, 25–26, 30, 36–38, 40, 52, 54–55, 64, 66, 71, 73, 75, 80–81, 85, 92, 103, 110–111, 113, 118–119
Lottery, The, 19, 120
Lovecraft, 18, 121
Lynch, David, 43, 121

M

manifestations, 5, 9, 18, 21, 33, 50–51, 54, 66, 89, 99
masks, 12, 52, 66, 68–69, 89
maternal horror, 15
Medak, Peter, 4, 30–31, 60, 83, 101, 111, 122
memory, 1, 9, 12, 18, 20, 23, 26–31, 33–37, 46, 54–58, 60–62, 66–68, 70, 93, 102, 112, 122, 124
metaphoric processing, 20, 30, 34, 35, 105, 110
microtrauma, 44
Midsommar, 22, 43, 83, 102, 103, 116
Mihalka, George, 83, 122
mirror, 14, 19, 30–31, 39–43, 79, 94, 107
Mirrors, 43, 94, 116
monster, 1–3, 5–6, 14–16, 18, 22, 28, 40, 43, 46, 49, 54–55, 58, 60, 64, 69, 72, 77, 80–81, 84, 87–89, 92–98, 100–102, 105, 107, 109, 110–111, 113, 114–115, 119
Muschietti, Andy, 31, 70, 82, 122
muteness, 56, 58

N

Nakata, Hideo, 16, 32, 76, 122
narrative, 4–6, 9–10, 14, 17–19, 24, 27–28, 32, 34, 40, 49, 54–56, 58, 60, 63–67, 70, 73, 79–80, 82–83, 88–89, 91–92, 94, 96, 100–102, 105, 110, 113, 115, 121
narrative collapse, 56
neuroscience of trauma, 3, 7, 13, 21–22, 27–29, 37, 56–57, 68–69, 70, 84, 107, 119, 121–122
Night House, The, 4, 83, 117
Night of the Living Dead, 17, 123

Nightmare on Elm Street, A, 19, 31, 61, 95–97, 100–101, 117
nightmares, 19, 36, 58

O

objects (preserved), 30–31
Occulus, 43
Others, The, 4, 54, 89, 116
overcoming, 5, 21–22, 79, 80, 95–97, 101–103, 106, 114, 125

P

Paranormal Activity, 101, 122
parent–child, 16
Peele, Jordan, 10, 19, 31, 85, 95, 101, 122
Peli, Oren, 101, 122
Pet Sematary, 37, 120–121
physical abuse, 52
Pizzolatto, Nic, 94
Polanski, Roman, 23, 43, 58, 67, 108, 122
Poltergeist, 43, 89–90, 101, 120
possession, 14, 43, 124
Possession, 22, 125
post-traumatic syndrome, 51
predictive processing, 7, 21, 30, 33, 105, 120
primary processing, 5
processing (of experience), 2–3, 5–8, 11, 13, 20–21, 23, 26–28, 30, 33–34, 37, 39, 44, 51, 56–57, 59–63, 66–67, 75, 79, 81–82, 84, 86, 90–91, 93, 99–101, 103, 105–106, 108–111, 113–114, 117, 119, 120, 122–123
projection, 14, 48
Psycho, 11, 15, 26, 30–31, 48, 65, 87, 98, 104, 112, 118, 120, 124
PTSD, 22–23, 27–28, 56–57, 70, 82, 107, 122

R

rage, 2, 13, 29, 37, 38, 41–42, 47, 52, 57, 68, 70, 75, 78, 120
Raimi, Sam, 92, 123
Real, the, 20, 26, 55, 58, 60, 65, 88, 92–93
recognition, 4, 6, 24–25, 41, 54–55, 81, 105
Red Dragon, 43, 123
re-emergence, 1–2, 4, 6, 19, 24, 49, 50–55, 57, 59, 61, 63, 65–69, 71, 73, 75, 77, 79–80, 84
Relic, 4, 120
repetition, 3–4, 24, 35, 44, 54–55, 63, 66, 68–69, 70–72, 76, 82, 89, 103, 119

Repulsion, 23, 43, 58, 67, 108, 122
resistance, 4, 28, 54–55, 79, 82, 85–87
revenge, 2, 22
Roeg, Nicolas, 36, 83, 111, 123
Rose, Bernard, 94
Run, 16, 26, 117

S

sacrifice/sacrificial, 22, 38, 77–78, 80, 96, 98, 100
Saint Maud, 59, 119
Salva, Victor, 83, 94, 123
Scott, Ridley, 29, 79–80, 95, 97, 101
security, 8, 14, 47, 109, 110, 122
self, 1, 4–6, 8–12, 14, 18, 23–25, 27–30, 33, 37–41, 43–45, 47, 49, 51, 53, 62, 65–67, 70–71, 77, 84, 87, 94, 96, 101, 112, 114, 119
shaman, 28, 60, 79–80, 90–95, 101
shame, 24–25, 32, 43–44, 71, 82, 101, 105, 116
Shining, The, 32, 43, 83, 94, 120
Shyamalan, M. Night, 4, 11, 44, 89, 123
sightings, 50–51, 54, 79, 82
Signs, 4, 123
Silence of the Lambs, The, 98, 118
silencing, 21, 24, 34, 88, 99
Sinister, 81, 89, 118
Skin I Live In, The, 38, 111, 116
Slender Man, 94, 124
society, 4–5, 8–10, 13, 15, 19, 22, 24–25, 31, 50, 54, 66, 83, 86, 88–89, 91, 94, 102
Spider, 46, 59, 118
Spielberg, Steven, 87, 90, 95, 98, 123
Split, 11, 44, 123
splitting, 32, 83
Sputnik, 29, 116
Stand, The, 17, 120
Stanley, Richard, 16, 18, 77, 123
storytelling, 79
Strange Case of Dr Jekyll and Mr Hyde, The, 10
symbolic efficacy, 91
symptoms, 3, 21–22, 50–51, 53–54, 66, 81–82, 84, 107

T

Talk to Me, 4, 48, 102, 122
Texas Chainsaw Massacre, The, 13, 79, 80, 100, 104, 120

therapy, 5–6, 22, 95, 105–106, 108–112, 114–115, 119
 allegorical moment, 111–112
 cathartic way, 106, 109
 evocative way, 106
 free association, 105–107
 from dissociation to conflict, 112–113
 objects of mourning, 110
 prescriptive way, 107, 113–114
 putting characters on the couch, 114–115
 thirdness, 111
 transitional phenomena/play, 109–110
 window of tolerance, 109–110, 114
thickening, 54
Thing, The, 14, 17, 82, 117, 122
Third, 25, 116
Thomas, Keith, 92, 124
trance, 79–80, 82, 95–96, 101, 103
traumatic memories, 20, 27, 35, 56–57
traumatic past, 30, 49, 51, 59, 62, 86
True Detective, 94
trust, 6–9, 14–15, 25, 34, 62, 64, 70, 97
Twin Peaks, 43, 121

U

uncanny, 10, 30–31, 37, 42, 69, 70, 77, 79, 82, 85, 119
unconscious, 5–7, 32, 66, 69, 70, 73, 80, 83, 91, 100, 103, 105–106
Under the Shadow, 94, 116
Under the Skin, 14, 119
unpeeling, 18, 19
unprocessed experience, 1–2, 4, 6, 31, 53, 109
Us, 10, 19, 31, 122
Uzumaki, 18, 120

V

Verbinski, Gore, 89, 124
victimization, 2, 69, 70, 115
Villaronga, Agustí, 43, 72, 124
voluntary exposure, 97, 101

W

Weekes, Remi, 4, 54–55, 79–80, 83, 87, 93, 124
What Ever Happened to Baby Jane?, 31, 116
White, Sylvain, 42, 90, 94, 124
Wise, Robert, 48–49, 83, 124
Witch, The, 104, 118
witness, 2, 5, 11, 17, 48, 52, 72, 102, 109

www.ingramcontent.com/pod-product-compliance
Ingram Content Group UK Ltd.
Pitfield, Milton Keynes, MK11 3LW, UK
UKHW030116300125
454373UK00012B/113